INTERNATIONAL THEOLOGICAL COMMISSION

SENSUS FIDEI
IN THE LIFE OF THE CHURCH

*All documents are published thanks to the generous support
of the members of the Catholic Truth Society*

CATHOLIC TRUTH SOCIETY
PUBLISHERS TO THE HOLY SEE

First published 2014 by The Incorporated Catholic Truth Society 40-46 Harleyford Road London SE11 5AY Tel: 020 7640 0042 Fax: 020 7640 0046. Libreria Editrice Vaticana omnia sibi vindicate iura. Sine eiusdem licentia scripto data nemini liceat hunc Sensus Fidei denuo imprimere aut in aliam linguam vertere. Copyright © 2014 Libreria Editrice Vaticana, Citta del Vaticano. Copyright © 2014 The Catholic Bishops' Conference of England and Wales.

ISBN 978 1 78469 023 6

CONTENTS

Introduction 5

CHAPTER ONE:
THE SENSUS FIDEI IN SCRIPTURE AND TRADITION

1. Biblical teaching 9

   a) Faith as response to the Word of God 9

   b) The personal and ecclesial dimensions of faith. 10

   c) The capacity of believers to know and witness to the truth 12

2. The development of the idea, and its place in the history of
   the Church 15

   a) Patristic period. 15

   b) Medieval period 17

   c) Reformation and post-Reformation period 19

   d) 19th century. 21

   e) 20th century. 25

CHAPTER TWO:
THE SENSUS FIDEI FIDELIS IN THE PERSONAL LIFE
OF THE BELIEVER

1. The *sensus fidei* as an instinct of faith. 31

2. Manifestations of the *sensus fidei* in the personal life of believers 35

CHAPTER THREE:
THE SENSUS FIDEI FIDELIUM IN THE LIFE OF THE CHURCH

1. The *sensus fidei* and the development of Christian doctrine
   and practice 39

   a) Retrospective and prospective aspects of the *sensus fidei*. 40

   b) The contribution of the laity to the *sensus fidelium* 41

2. The *sensus fidei* and the magisterium 42

   a) The magisterium listens to the *sensus fidelium* 42

   b) The magisterium nurtures, discerns and judges the
     sensus fidelium 43

   c) Reception. 44

3. The *sensus fidei* and theology 45

   a) Theologians depend on the *sensus fidelium* 46

   b) Theologians reflect on the *sensus fidelium* 47

4. Ecumenical aspects of the *sensus fidei* 47

CHAPTER FOUR:
HOW TO DISCERN AUTHENTIC MANIFESTATIONS
OF THE SENSUS FIDEI

1. Dispositions needed for authentic participation in the *sensus fidei* 49

   a) Participation in the life of the Church 50

   b) Listening to the word of God 50

   c) Openness to reason 51

   d) Adherence to the magisterium. 51

   e) Holiness – humility, freedom and joy 52

   f) Seeking the edification of the Church 54

2. Applications. 54

   a) The *sensus fidei* and popular religiosity 54

   b) The *sensus fidei* and public opinion 57

   c) Ways of consulting the faithful 60

Conclusion 63

* PRELIMINARY NOTE

In its quinquennium of 2009-2014, the International Theological Commission studied the nature of *sensus fidei* and its place in the life of the Church. The work took place in a subcommission presided by Msgr. Paul McPartlan and composed of the following members: Fr. Serge Thomas Bonino, O.P. (Secretary General); Sr. Sara Butler, M.S.B.T.; Rev. Antonio Castellano, S.D.B.; Rev. Adelbert Denaux; Msgr. Tomislav Ivančić; Bishop Jan Liesen; Rev. Leonard Santedi Kinkupu, Doctor Thomas Söding, and Msgr. Jerzy Szymik.

The general discussions of this theme were held in numerous meetings of the subcommission and during the Plenary Sessions of the same International Theological Commission held in Rome between 2011 and 2014. The text "*Sensus fidei* in the Life of the Church" was approved in *forma specifica* by the majority of members of commission, by a written vote, and was then submitted to its President, Cardinal Gerhard L. Müller, Prefect of the Congregation for the Doctrine of the Faith, who authorized its publication.

INTRODUCTION

1. By the gift of the Holy Spirit, 'the Spirit of truth who comes from the Father' and bears witness to the Son (*Jn* 15:26), all of the baptised participate in the prophetic office of Jesus Christ, 'the faithful and true witness' (*Rv* 3:14). They are to bear witness to the Gospel and to the apostolic faith in the Church and in the world. The Holy Spirit anoints them and equips them for that high calling, conferring on them a very personal and intimate knowledge of the faith of the Church. In the first letter of St John, the faithful are told: 'you have been anointed by the Holy One, and all of you have knowledge', 'the anointing that you received from [Christ] abides in you, and so you do not need anyone to teach you', 'his anointing teaches you about all things' (*1 Jn* 2:20, 27).

2. As a result, the faithful have an instinct for the truth of the Gospel, which enables them to recognise and endorse authentic Christian doctrine and practice, and to reject what is false. That supernatural instinct, intrinsically linked to the gift of faith received in the communion of the Church, is called the *sensus fidei*, and it enables Christians to fulfil their prophetic calling. In his first Angelus address, Pope Francis quoted the words of a humble, elderly woman he once met: 'If the Lord did not forgive everything, the world would not exist'; and he commented with admiration: 'that is the wisdom which the Holy Spirit gives'.[1] The woman's insight is a striking manifestation of the *sensus fidei*, which, as well as enabling a certain discernment with regard to the things of faith, fosters true wisdom and gives rise, as here, to proclamation of the truth. It is clear, therefore, that the *sensus fidei* is a vital resource for the new evangelisation to which the Church is strongly committed in our time.[2]

3. As a theological concept, the *sensus fidei* refers to two realities which are distinct though closely connected, the proper subject of one being the Church, 'pillar and bulwark of the truth' (*1 Tm* 3:15),[3] while the subject

---

[1] POPE FRANCIS, Angelus address, 17 March, 2013.

[2] Cf. POPE FRANCIS, Apostolic Exhortation, *Evangelii Gaudium* (2013), nn.119-120.

[3] Biblical quotations are from the New Revised Standard Version. Unless otherwise indicated,

of the other is the individual believer, who belongs to the Church through the sacraments of initiation, and who, by means of regular celebration of the Eucharist in particular, participates in her faith and life. On the one hand, the *sensus fidei* refers to the personal capacity of the believer, within the communion of the Church, to discern the truth of faith. On the other hand, the *sensus fidei* refers to a communal and ecclesial reality: the instinct of faith of the Church herself, by which she recognises her Lord and proclaims his word. The *sensus fidei* in this sense is reflected in the convergence of the baptised in a lived adhesion to a doctrine of faith or to an element of Christian praxis. This convergence (*consensus*) plays a vital role in the Church: the *consensus fidelium* is a sure criterion for determining whether a particular doctrine or practice belongs to the apostolic faith.[4] In the present document, we use the term, *sensus fidei fidelis*, to refer to the personal aptitude of the believer to make an accurate discernment in matters of faith, and *sensus fidei fidelium* to refer to the Church's own instinct of faith. According to the context, *sensus fidei* refers to either the former or the latter, and in the latter case the term, *sensus fidelium*, is also used.

4. The importance of the *sensus fidei* in the life of the Church was strongly emphasised by the Second Vatican Council. Banishing the caricature of an active hierarchy and a passive laity, and in particular the notion of a strict separation between the teaching Church (*Ecclesia docens*) and the learning Church (*Ecclesia discens*), the council taught

---

quotations from the documents of the Second Vatican Council are taken from Austin Flannery, ed., *Vatican Council II*, new revised edition (Northport, NY/Dublin: Costello Publishing Company/Dominican Publications, 1996). The following council documents will be identified as shown: *Apostolicam Actuositatem* (AA), *Ad Gentes* (AG), *Dei Verbum* (DV), *Gaudium et Spes* (GS), *Lumen Gentium* (LG), *Perfectae Caritatis* (PC), *Sacrosanctum Concilium* (SC). References to Heinrich Denzinger, *Enchiridion symbolorum definitionum et declarationum de rebus fidei et morum,* 38th ed., edited by Peter Hünermann (1999), are indicated by DH together with the paragraph number; references to the *Catechism of the Catholic Church* (1992) are indicated by CCC together with the paragraph number; and references to J. P. Migne, ed., *Patrologia Latina* (1844-1864) are indicated by PL together with the volume and column numbers.

[4] In its document on *The Interpretation of Dogma* (1989), the International Theological Commission (ITC) spoke of the '*sensus fidelium*' as an 'inner sense' by means of which the people of God 'recognise in preaching that the words are God's not man's and accept and guard them with unbreakable fidelity' (C, II, 1). The document also highlighted the role played by the *consensus fidelium* in the interpretation of dogma (C, II, 4).

that all the baptised participate in their own proper way in the three offices of Christ as prophet, priest and king. In particular, it taught that Christ fulfills his prophetic office not only by means of the hierarchy but also via the laity.

5. In the reception and application of the council's teaching on this topic, however, many questions arise, especially in relation to controversies regarding various doctrinal or moral issues. What exactly is the *sensus fidei* and how can it be identified? What are the biblical sources for this idea and how does the *sensus fidei* function in the tradition of the faith? How does the *sensus fidei* relate to the ecclesiastical magisterium of the pope and the bishops, and to theology?[5] What are the conditions for an authentic exercise of the *sensus fidei*? Is the *sensus fidei* something different from the majority opinion of the faithful in a given time or place, and if so how does it differ from the latter? All of these questions require answers if the idea of the *sensus fidei* is to be understood more fully and used more confidently in the Church today.

6. The purpose of the present text is not to give an exhaustive account of the *sensus fidei*, but simply to clarify and deepen some important aspects of this vital notion in order to respond to certain issues, particularly regarding how to identify the authentic *sensus fidei* in situations of controversy, when for example there are tensions between the teaching of the magisterium and views claiming to express the *sensus fidei*. Accordingly, it will first consider the biblical sources for the idea of the *sensus fidei* and the way in which this idea has developed and functioned in the history and tradition of the Church (chapter one). The nature of the *sensus fidei fidelis* will then be considered, together with the manifestations of the latter in the personal life of the believer (chapter two). The document will then reflect on the *sensus fidei fidelium*, that is, the *sensus fidei* in its ecclesial form, considering first its role in the development of Christian doctrine and practice, then its relationship to the magisterium and to theology, respectively, and then also its importance for ecumenical dialogue (chapter three). Finally, it will seek to identify

---

[5] In its recent document entitled *Theology Today: Perspectives, Principles and Criteria* (2012), the ITC identified the *sensus fidei* as a fundamental locus or reference point for theology (n.35).

dispositions needed for an authentic participation in the *sensus fidei* – they constitute criteria for a discernment of the authentic *sensus fidei* – and will reflect on some applications of its findings to the concrete life of the Church (chapter four).

CHAPTER ONE

THE SENSUS FIDEI IN SCRIPTURE AND TRADITION

7. The phrase, *sensus fidei*, is found neither in the Scriptures nor in the formal teaching of the Church until Vatican II. However, the idea that the Church as a whole is infallible in her belief, since she is the body and bride of Christ (cf. *1 Co* 12:27; *Ep* 4:12; 5:21-32; *Rv* 21:9), and that all of her members have an anointing that teaches them (cf. *1 Jn* 2:20, 27), being endowed with the Spirit of truth (cf. *Jn* 16:13), is everywhere apparent from the very beginnings of Christianity. The present chapter will trace the main lines of the development of this idea, first in Scripture and then in the subsequent history of the Church.

1. BIBLICAL TEACHING

a) Faith as response to the Word of God

8. Throughout the New Testament, faith is the fundamental and decisive response of human persons to the Gospel. Jesus proclaims the Gospel in order to bring people to faith: 'The time is fulfilled, and the kingdom of God has come near; repent, and believe in the good news' (*Mk* 1:15). Paul reminds the early Christians of his apostolic proclamation of the death and resurrection of Jesus Christ in order to renew and deepen their faith: 'Now I would remind you, brothers and sisters, of the good news that I proclaimed to you, which you in turn received, in which also you stand, through which also you are being saved, if you hold firmly to the message that I proclaimed to you – unless you have come to believe in vain' (*1 Co* 15:1-2). The understanding of faith in the New Testament is rooted in the Old Testament, and especially in the faith of Abram, who trusted completely in God's promises (*Gn* 15:6; cf. *Rm* 4:11, 17). This faith is a free answer to the proclamation of the word of God, and as such it is a gift of the Holy Spirit to be received by those who truly believe (cf. *1 Co* 12:3). The 'obedience of faith' (*Rm* 1:5) is the result of God's grace, who frees human beings and gives them membership in the Church (*Ga* 5:1,13).

9. The Gospel calls forth faith because it is not simply the conveying of religious information but the proclamation of the word of God, and 'the power of God for salvation', which is truly to be received (*Rm* 1:16-17; cf. *Mt* 11:15; *Lk* 7:22 [*Is* 26:19; 29:18; 35:5-6; 61:1-11]). It is the Gospel of God's grace (*Ac* 20:24), the 'revelation of the mystery' of God (*Rm* 16:25), and the 'word of truth' (*Ep* 1:13). The Gospel has a substantial content: the coming of God's Kingdom, the resurrection and exaltation of the crucified Jesus Christ, the mystery of salvation and glorification by God in the Holy Spirit. The Gospel has a strong subject: Jesus himself, the Word of God, who sends out his apostles and their followers, and it takes the direct form of inspired and authorised proclamation by words and deeds. To receive the Gospel requires a response of the whole person 'with all your heart, and with all your soul, and with all your mind, and with all your strength' (*Mk* 12:31). This is the response of faith, which is 'the assurance of things hoped for, the conviction of things not seen' (*Heb* 11:1).

10. '"Faith" is both an act of belief or trust and also that which is believed or confessed, *fides qua* and *fides quae*, respectively. Both aspects work together inseparably, since trust is adhesion to a message with intelligible content, and confession cannot be reduced to mere lip service, it must come from the heart.'[6] The Old and New Testaments clearly show that the form and content of faith belong together.

b) The personal and ecclesial dimensions of faith

11. The scriptures show that the personal dimension of faith is integrated into the ecclesial dimension; both singular and plural forms of the first person are found: 'we believe' (cf. *Ga* 2:16) and 'I believe' (cf. *Ga* 2:19-20). In his letters, Paul recognises the faith of believers as both a personal and an ecclesial reality. He teaches that everyone who confesses that 'Jesus is Lord' is inspired by the Holy Spirit (*1 Co* 12:3). The Spirit incorporates every believer into the body of Christ and gives him or her a special role in order to build up the Church (cf. *1 Co* 12:4-27). In the letter to the Ephesians, confession of the one and only God is connected with the reality of a life of faith in the Church: 'There is one body and one Spirit, just as you were called to the one hope of your calling, one Lord,

---

[6] *Theology Today,* §13.

one faith, one baptism, one God and Father of all, who is above all and through all and in all' (*Ep* 4:4-6).

12. In its personal and ecclesial dimensions, faith has the following essential aspects:

i) Faith requires repentance. In the proclamation of the prophets of Israel and of John the Baptist (cf. *Mk* 1:4), as well as in the preaching of the Good News by Jesus himself (*Mk* 1:14f.) and in the mission of the Apostles (*Ac* 2:38-42; *1 Th* 1:9f.), repentance means the confession of one's sins and the beginning of a new life lived within the community of the covenant of God (cf. *Rm* 12:1f.).

ii) Faith is both expressed in and nourished by prayer and worship (*leitourgia*). Prayer can take various forms – begging, imploring, praising, thanksgiving – and the confession of faith is a special form of prayer. Liturgical prayer, and pre-eminently the celebration of the Eucharist, has from the very beginning been essential to the life of the Christian community (cf. *Ac* 2:42). Prayer takes place both in public (cf. *1 Co* 14) and in private (cf. *Mt* 6:5). For Jesus, the Our Father (*Mt* 6:9-13; *Lk* 11:1-4) expresses the essence of faith. It is a 'summary of the whole Gospel'.[7] Significantly, its language is that of 'we', 'us' and 'our'.

iii) Faith brings knowledge. The one who believes is able to recognise the truth of God (cf. *Ph* 3:10f.). Such knowledge springs from reflection on the experience of God, based on revelation and shared in the community of believers. This is the witness of both Old and New Testament Wisdom theology (*Ps* 111:10; cf. *Pr* 1:7; 9:10; *Mt* 11:27; *Lk* 10:22).

iv) Faith leads to confession (*marturia*). Inspired by the Holy Spirit, believers know the one in whom they have placed their trust (cf. *2 Tm* 1:12), and are able to give an account of the hope that is in them (cf. *1 Pt* 3:15), thanks to the prophetic and apostolic proclamation of the Gospel (cf. *Rm* 10:9f.). They do that in their own name; but they do it from within the communion of believers.

---

[7] TERTULLIAN, *De oratione*, I, 6; *Corpus Christianorum, series latina* (hereafter CCSL), 1, p.258.

v) Faith involves confidence. To trust in God means to base one's whole life on the promise of God. In Heb 11, many Old Testament believers are mentioned as members of a great procession through time and space to God in heaven, guided by Jesus the 'the pioneer and perfecter of our faith' (*Heb* 12:3). Christians are part of this procession, sharing the same hope and conviction (*Heb* 11:1), and already 'surrounded by so great a cloud of witnesses' (*Heb* 12:1).

vi) Faith entails responsibility, and especially charity and service (*diakonia*). The disciples will be known 'by their fruits' (*Mt* 7:20). The fruits belong essentially to faith, because faith, which comes from listening to the word of God, requires obedience to his will. The faith which justifies (*Ga* 2:16) is 'faith working through love' (*Ga* 5:6; cf. *Jas* 2:21-24). Love for one's brother and sister is in fact the criterion for love of God (1 *Jn* 4:20).

c) The capacity of believers to know and witness to the truth

13. In Jeremiah, a 'new covenant' is promised, one which will involve the internalisation of God's word: 'I will put my law within them, and I will write it on their hearts; and I will be their God, and they shall be my people. No longer shall they teach one another, or say to each other, "Know the Lord", for they shall all know me, from the least of them to the greatest, says the Lord; for I will forgive their iniquity, and remember their sin no more' (*Jr* 31:33-34). The people of God is to be created anew, receiving 'a new spirit', so as to be able to recognise the law and to follow it (*Ez* 11:19-20). This promise is fulfilled in the ministry of Jesus and the life of the Church by the gift of the Holy Spirit. It is especially fulfilled in the celebration of the Eucharist, where the faithful receive the cup that is 'the new covenant' in the Lord's blood (*Lk* 22:20; *1 Co* 11:25; cf. *Rm* 11:27; *Heb* 8:6-12; 10:14-17).

14. In his farewell discourse, in the context of the Last Supper, Jesus promised his disciples the 'Advocate', the Spirit of truth (*Jn* 14:16, 26; 15:26; 16:7-14). The Spirit will remind them of the words of Jesus (*Jn* 14:26), enable them to testify to the word of God (*Jn* 15:26-27), 'prove the world wrong about sin and righteousness and judgement' (*Jn* 16:8), and 'guide' the disciples 'into all the truth' (*Jn* 16:13). All of this happens thanks to the gift of the Spirit through the paschal mystery, celebrated in

the life of the Christian community, particularly in the Eucharist, until the Lord comes (cf. *1 Co* 11:26). The disciples have an inspired sense for the ever-actual truth of God's word incarnate in Jesus and of its meaning for today (cf. *2 Co* 6:2), and that is what drives the people of God, guided by the Holy Spirit, to bear witness to their faith in the Church and in the world.

15. Moses wished that all of the people might be prophets by receiving the spirit of the Lord (*Nu* 11:29). That wish became an eschatological promise through the prophet, Joel, and at Pentecost Peter proclaims the fulfilment of the promise: 'In the last days it will be, God declares, that I will pour out my Spirit upon all flesh, and your sons and your daughters shall prophesy' (*Ac* 2:17; cf. *Jl* 3:1). The Spirit who was promised (cf. *Ac* 1:8) is poured out, enabling the faithful to speak 'about God's deeds of power' (*Ac* 2:11).

16. The first description of the community of believers in Jerusalem combines four elements: 'They devoted themselves to the apostles' teaching and fellowship, to the breaking of bread and the prayers' (Ac 2:42). Devotion to these four elements powerfully manifests apostolic faith. Faith clings to the authentic teaching of the Apostles, which remembers the teaching of Jesus (cf. *Lk* 1:1-4); it draws believers into fellowship with one another; it is renewed through the encounter with the Lord in the breaking of bread; and it is nourished in prayer.

17. When in the church of Jerusalem a conflict arose between the Hellenists and the Hebrews about the daily distribution, the twelve apostles summoned 'the whole community of the disciples' and took a decision that 'pleased the whole community'. The whole community chose 'seven men of good standing, full of the Spirit and of wisdom', and set them before the apostles who then prayed and laid their hands upon them (*Ac* 6:1-6). When problems arose in the church of Antioch concerning circumcision and the practice of the Torah, the case was submitted to the judgement of the mother church of Jerusalem. The resulting apostolic council was of the greatest importance for the future of the Church. Luke describes the sequence of events carefully. The 'apostles and the elders met together to consider this matter' (*Ac* 15:6). Peter told the story of his being inspired by the Holy Spirit to baptise Cornelius and his house even though they were uncircumcised

(*Ac* 15:7-11). Paul and Barnabas told of their missionary experience in the local church of Antioch (*Ac* 15:12; cf. 15:1-5). James reflected on those experiences in the light of the Scriptures (*Ac* 15:13-18), and proposed a decision that favoured the unity of the Church (*Ac* 15:19-21). 'Then the apostles and the elders, with the consent of the whole church, decided to choose men from among their members and to send them to Antioch with Paul and Barnabas' (*Ac* 15:22). The letter which communicated the decision was received by the community with the joy of faith (*Ac* 15:23-33). For Luke, these events demonstrated proper ecclesial action, involving both the pastoral service of the apostles and elders and also the participation of the community, qualified to participate by their faith.

18. Writing to the Corinthians, Paul identifies the foolishness of the cross as the wisdom of God (*1 Co* 1:18-25). Explaining how this paradox is comprehensible, he says: 'we have the mind of Christ' (*1 Co* 2:16; ἡ μεῖς δέ νοῦν Χριστοῦ εχομεν; *nos autem sensum Christi habemus*, in the Vulgate). 'We' here refers to the church of Corinth in communion with her Apostle as part of the whole community of believers (*1 Co* 1:1-2). The capacity to recognise the crucified Messiah as the wisdom of God is given by the Holy Spirit; it is not a privilege of the wise and the scribes (cf. *1 Co* 1:20), but is given to the poor, the marginalised, and to those who are 'foolish' in the eyes of the world (*1 Co* 1:26-29). Even so, Paul criticises the Corinthians for being 'still of the flesh', still not ready for 'solid food' (*1 Co* 3:1-4). Their faith needs to mature and to find better expression in their words and deeds.

19. In his own ministry, Paul shows respect for, and a desire to deepen, the faith of his communities. In 2 Co 1:24, he describes his mission as an apostle in the following terms: 'I do not mean to imply that we lord it over your faith; rather, we are workers with you for your joy, because you stand firm in the faith', and he encourages the Corinthians: 'Stand firm in your faith' (*1 Co* 16:14). To the Thessalonians, he writes a letter 'to strengthen and encourage you for the sake of your faith' (*1 Th* 3:2), and he prays for the faith of other communities likewise (cf. *Col* 1:9; *Ep* 1:17-19). The apostle not only works for an increase in the faith of others, he knows his own faith to be strengthened thereby in a sort of dialogue of faith: '... that we may be mutually encouraged by each other's faith, both yours and mine' (*Rm* 1:17). The faith of the community

is a reference point for Paul's teaching and a focus for his pastoral service, giving rise to a mutually beneficial interchange between him and his communities.

20. In the first letter of John, the apostolic Tradition is mentioned (*1 Jn* 1:1-4), and the readers are reminded of their baptism: 'You have been anointed by the Holy One, and all of you have knowledge' (*1 Jn* 2:20). The letter continues: 'As for you, the anointing that you received from him abides in you, and so you do not need anyone to teach you. But as his anointing teaches you about all things, and is true and is not a lie, and just as it has taught you, abide in him' (*1 Jn* 2:27).

21. Finally, in the Book of Revelation, John the prophet repeats in all of his letters to the churches (cf. *Rv* 2-3) the formula: 'Let anyone who has an ear listen to what the Spirit is saying to the churches' (*Rv* 2:7, et al.). The members of the churches are charged to heed the living word of the Spirit, to receive it, and to give glory to God. It is by the obedience of faith, itself a gift of the Spirit, that the faithful are able to recognise the teaching they are receiving truly as the teaching of the same Spirit, and to respond to the instructions they are given.

2. THE DEVELOPMENT OF THE IDEA, AND ITS PLACE IN THE HISTORY OF THE CHURCH

22. The concept of the *sensus fidelium* began to be elaborated and used in a more systematic way at the time of the Reformation, though the decisive role of the *consensus fidelium* in the discernment and development of doctrine concerning faith and morals was already recognised in the patristic and medieval periods. What was still needed, however, was more attention to the specific role of the laity in this regard. That issue received attention particularly from the nineteenth century onwards.

a) Patristic period

23. The Fathers and theologians of the first few centuries considered the faith of the whole Church to be a sure point of reference for discerning the content of the apostolic Tradition. Their conviction about the solidity and even the infallibility of the discernment of the whole Church on matters of faith and morals was expressed in the context of controversy. They refuted the dangerous novelties introduced by heretics by comparing them with

what was held and done in all the churches.[8] For Tertullian (c.160-c.225), the fact that all the churches have substantially the same faith testifies to Christ's presence and the guidance of the Holy Spirit; those go astray who abandon the faith of the whole Church.[9] For Augustine (354-430), the whole Church, 'from the bishops to the least of the faithful', bears witness to the truth.[10] The general consent of Christians functions as a sure norm for determining the apostolic faith: '*Securus iudicat orbis terrarum* [the judgement of the whole world is sure]'.[11] John Cassian (c.360-435) held that the universal consent of the faithful is a sufficient argument to confute heretics,[12] and Vincent of Lérins (died c.445) proposed as a norm the faith that was held everywhere, always, and by everyone (*quod ubique, quod semper, quod ab omnibus creditum est*).[13]

24. To resolve disputes among the faithful, the Church Fathers appealed not only to common belief but also to the constant tradition of practice. Jerome (c.345-420), for example, found justification for the veneration of relics by pointing to the practice of the bishops and of the faithful,[14] and Epiphanius (c.315-403), in defence of Mary's perpetual virginity, asked whether anyone had ever dared to utter her name without adding 'the Virgin'.[15]

25. The testimony of the patristic period chiefly concerns the prophetic witness of the people of God as a whole, something that has a certain

---

[8] YVES M.-J. CONGAR identifies various doctrinal questions in which the *sensus fidelium* was used in *Jalons pour une Théologie du Laïcat* (Paris: Éditions du Cerf, 1953), 450-53; ET: *Lay People in the Church: A Study for a Theology of Lay People* (London: Chapman, 1965), Appendix II: The '*Sensus fidelium*' in the Fathers, 465-67.

[9] TERTULLIAN, *De praescriptione haereticorum*, 21 and 28, CCSL 1, pp.202-203 and 209.

[10] AUGUSTINE, *De praedestinatione sanctorum*, XIV, 27 (PL 44, 980). He says this with reference to the canonicity of the book of Wisdom.

[11] AUGUSTINE, *Contra epistolam Parmeniani*, III, 24 (PL 43, 101). Cf. *De baptismo*, IV, xxiv, 31 (PL 43, 174) (with regard to the baptism of infants): 'Quod universa tenet Ecclesia, nec conciliis institutum, sed semper retentum est, nonnisi auctoritate apostolica traditum rectissime creditur'.

[12] CASSIAN, *De incarnatione Christi*, I, 6 (PL 50, 29-30): 'Sufficere ergo solus nunc ad confutandum haeresim deberet consensus omnium, quia indubitatae veritatis manifestatio est auctoritas universorum'.

[13] VINCENT OF LÉRINS, *Commonitorium* II, 5 (CCSL, 64, p.149).

[14] JEROME, *Adversus Vigilantium* 5 (CCSL 79C, p.11-13).

[15] EPIPHANIUS OF SALAMIS, *Panarion haereticorum*, 78, 6; Die griechischen christlichen Schriftsteller der ersten Jahrhunderte, Epiphanius, Bd 3, p.456.

16

objective character. The believing people as a whole cannot err in matters of faith, it was claimed, because they have received an anointing from Christ, the promised Holy Spirit, which equips them to discern the truth. Some Fathers of the Church also reflected on the subjective capacity of Christians animated by faith and indwelt by the Holy Spirit to maintain true doctrine in the Church and to reject error. Augustine, for example, called attention to this when he asserted that Christ 'the interior Teacher' enables the laity as well as their pastors not only to receive the truth of revelation but also to approve and transmit it.[16]

26. In the first five centuries, the faith of the Church as a whole proved decisive in determining the canon of Scripture and in defining major doctrines concerning, for example, the divinity of Christ, the perpetual virginity and divine motherhood of Mary, and the veneration and invocation of the saints. In some cases, as Blessed John Henry Newman (1801-90) remarked, the faith of the laity, in particular, played a crucial role. The most striking example was in the famous controversy in the fourth century with the Arians, who were condemned at the Council of Nicaea (325 AD), where the divinity of Jesus Christ was defined. From then until the Council of Constantinople (381 AD), however, there continued to be uncertainty among the bishops. During that period, 'the divine tradition committed to the infallible Church was proclaimed and maintained far more by the faithful than by the Episcopate'. '[T]here was a temporary suspense of the functions of the "*Ecclesia docens*". The body of Bishops failed in their confession of the faith. They spoke variously, one against another; there was nothing, after Nicaea, of firm, unvarying, consistent testimony, for nearly sixty years.'[17]

b) Medieval period

27. Newman also commented that 'in a later age, when the learned Benedictines of Germany [cf. Rabanus Maurus, c.780-856] and France

---

[16] AUGUSTINE, *In Iohannis Evangelium tractatus*, XX, 3 (CCSL 36, p.204); *Ennaratio in psalmum 120*, 7 (PL 37, 1611).

[17] JOHN HENRY NEWMAN, *On Consulting the Faithful in Matters of Doctrine*, edited with an introduction by John Coulson (London: Geoffrey Chapman, 1961), pp.75-101; at 75 and 77. See also his *The Arians of the Fourth Century* (1833; 3rd ed. 1871). Congar expresses some caution with regard to the use of Newman's analysis of this matter; see, CONGAR, *Jalons pour une Théologie du Laïcat*, p.395; ET: *Lay People in the Church*, pp.285-6.

[cf. Ratramnus, died c.870] were perplexed in their enunciation of the doctrine of the Real Presence, Paschasius [c.790-c.860] was supported by the faithful in his maintenance of it.'[18] Something similar happened with respect to the dogma, defined by Pope Benedict XII in the constitution, *Benedictus Deus* (1336), regarding the beatific vision, enjoyed already by souls after purgatory and before the day of judgement:[19] 'the tradition, on which the definition was made, was manifested in the *consensus fidelium*, with a luminousness which the succession of Bishops, though many of them were *"Sancti Patres ab ipsis Apostolorum temporibus"*, did not furnish'. '[M]ost considerable deference was paid to the *"sensus fidelium"*; their opinion and advice indeed was not asked, but their testimony was taken, their feelings consulted, their impatience, I had almost said, feared.'[20] The continuing development, among the faithful, of belief in, and devotion to, the Immaculate Conception of the Blessed Virgin Mary, in spite of opposition to the doctrine by certain theologians, is another major example of the role played in the Middle Ages by the *sensus fidelium*.

28. The Scholastic doctors acknowledged that the Church, the *congregatio fidelium*, cannot err in matters of faith because she is taught by God, united with Christ her Head, and indwelt by the Holy Spirit. Thomas Aquinas, for example, takes this as a premise on the grounds that the universal Church is governed by the Holy Spirit who, as the Lord Jesus promised, would teach her 'all truth' (*Jn* 16:13).[21] He knew that the faith of the universal Church is authoritatively expressed by her prelates,[22] but he was also particularly interested in each believer's personal instinct of faith, which he explored in relation to the theological virtue of faith.

---

[18] NEWMAN, *On Consulting the Faithful*, p.104.

[19] See DH 1000.

[20] NEWMAN, *On Consulting the Faithful*, p.70.

[21] THOMAS AQUINAS, *Summa theologiae*, IIa-IIae, q.1, a.9, s.c.; IIIa, q.83, a.5, s.c. (with regard to the liturgy of the Mass); *Quodl.* IX, q.8 (with regard to canonisation). Cf. also BONAVENTURE, *Commentaria in IV librum Sententiarum*, d.4, p.2, dub. 2 (Opera omnia, vol.4, Quaracchi, 1889, p.105): '[Fides Ecclesiae militantis] quamvis possit deficere in aliquibus personis specialiter, generaliter tamen numquam deficit nec deficiet, iuxta illud Matthaei ultimo: "Ecce ego vobiscum sum usque ad consumationem saeculi"'; d.18, p.2, a. un. q.4 (p.490). In *Summa theologiae*, IIa-IIae, q.2, a.6, ad 3, St Thomas links this indefectibility of the universal Church to Jesus's promise to Peter that his faith would not fail (*Lk* 22:32).

[22] *Summa theologiae*, IIa-IIae, q.1, a.10; q.11, a.2, ad 3.

c) Reformation and post-Reformation period

29. The challenge posed by the 16th century Reformers required renewed attention to the *sensus fidei fidelium*, and the first systematic treatment of it was worked out as a result. The Reformers emphasised the primacy of the word of God in Sacred Scripture (*Scriptura sola*) and the priesthood of the faithful. In their view, the internal testimony of the Holy Spirit gives all of the baptised the ability to interpret, by themselves, God's word; this conviction did not discourage them, however, from teaching in synods and producing catechisms for the instruction of the faithful. Their doctrines called into question, among other things, the role and status of Tradition, the authority of the pope and the bishops to teach, and the inerrancy of councils. In response to their claim that the promise of Christ's presence and the guidance of the Holy Spirit was given to the whole Church, not only to the Twelve but also to every believer,[23] Catholic theologians were led to explain more fully how the pastors serve the faith of the people. In the process, they gave increasing attention to the teaching authority of the hierarchy.

30. Theologians of the Catholic Reformation, building on previous efforts to develop a systematic ecclesiology, took up the question of revelation, its sources, and their authority. At first, they responded to the Reformers' critique of certain doctrines by appealing to the infallibility of the whole Church, laity and clergy together, in *credendo*.[24] The Council of Trent, in fact, repeatedly appealed to the judgement of the whole Church in its defence of disputed articles of Catholic doctrine. Its Decree on the Sacrament of the Eucharist (1551), for example, specifically invoked 'the universal understanding of the Church [*universum Ecclesiae sensum*]'.[25]

31. Melchior Cano (1509-1560), who attended the council, provided the first extended treatment of the *sensus fidei fidelium* in his defence of Catholic esteem for the probative force of Tradition in theological argument. In his

---

[23] See MARTIN LUTHER, *De captivitate Babylonica ecclesiae praecludium*, WA 6, 566-567, and John Calvin, *Institutio christianae religionis*, IV, 8, 11; the promises of Christ are found in Mt 28:19 and Jn 14: 16, 17.

[24] See GUSTAV THILS, *L'Infaillibilité du Peuple chrétien 'in credendo': Notes de théologie post-tridentine* (Paris: Desclée de Brouwer, 1963).

[25] DH 1637; see also, DH 1726. For equivalent expressions, see YVES M.-J. CONGAR, *La Tradition et les traditions*, II. *Essai théologique* (Paris: Fayard, 1963), pp.82-83; ET, *Tradition and Traditions* (London: Burns & Oates, 1966), 315-17.

treatise, *De locis theologicis* (1564),[26] he identified the present common consent of the faithful as one of four criteria for determining whether a doctrine or practice belongs to the apostolic tradition.[27] In a chapter on the Church's authority with respect to doctrine, he argued that the faith of the Church cannot fail because she is the Spouse (*Hos* 2; *1 Co* 11:2) and Body of Christ (*Ep* 5), and because the Holy Spirit guides her (*Jn* 14:16, 26).[28] Cano also noted that the word 'Church' sometimes designates all of the faithful, including the pastors, and sometimes designates her leaders and pastors (*principes et pastores*), for they too possess the Holy Spirit.[29] He used the word in the first sense when he asserted that the Church's faith cannot fail, that the Church cannot be deceived in believing, and that infallibility belongs not only to the Church of past ages but also to the Church as it is presently constituted. He used 'Church' in the second sense when he taught that her pastors are infallible in giving authoritative doctrinal judgements, for they are assisted in this task by the Holy Spirit (*Ep* 4; *1 Tm* 3).[30]

32. Robert Bellarmine (1542-1621), defending the Catholic faith against its Reformation critics, took the visible Church, the 'universality of all believers', as his starting point. For him, all that the faithful hold as *de fide*, and all that the bishops teach as pertaining to the faith, is necessarily true and to be believed.[31] He maintained that the councils of

---

[26] *De locis theologicis*, ed. JUAN BELDA PLANS (Madrid, 2006). Cano lists ten loci: Sacra Scriptura, traditiones Christi et apostolorum, Ecclesia Catholica, Concilia, Ecclesia Romana, sancti veteres, theologi scholastici, ratio naturalis, philosophi, humana historia.

[27] *De locis theol.*, Bk. IV, ch. 3 (Plans ed., p.117). 'Si quidquam est nunc in Ecclesia communi fidelium consensione probatum, quod tamen humana potestas efficere non potuit, id ex apostolorum traditione necessario derivatum est.'

[28] *De locis theol.*, Bk. I, ch. 4 (pp.144-46).

[29] *De locis theol.*, Bk. I, ch. 4 (p.149): 'Non solum Ecclesia universalis, id est, collectio omnium fidelium hunc veritatis spiritum semper habet, sed eundem habent etiam Ecclesiae principes et pastores'. In Book VI, Cano affirms the authority of the Roman pontiff when he defines a doctrine *ex cathedra*.

[30] *De locis theol.*, Bk. I, ch. 4 (pp.150-51): 'Priores itaque conclusiones illud astruebant, quicquid ecclesia, hoc est, omnium fidelium concio teneret, id verum esse. Haec autem illud affirmat pastores ecclesiae doctores in fide errare non posse, sed quicquid fidelem populum docent, quod ad Christi fidem attineat, esse verissimum.'

[31] ROBERT BELLARMINE, *De controversiis christianae fidei* (Venice, 1721), II, I, lib.3, cap.14: 'Et cum dicimus Ecclesiam non posse errare, id intelligimus tam de universitate fidelium quam de universitate Episcoporum, ita ut sensus sit eius propositionis, ecclesia non potest errare, idest, id

the Church cannot fail because they possess this *consensus Ecclesiae universalis*.[32]

33. Other theologians of the post-Tridentine era continued to affirm the infallibility of the *Ecclesia* (by which they meant the entire Church, inclusive of her pastors) *in credendo*, but began to distinguish the roles of the 'teaching Church' and the 'learning Church' rather sharply. The earlier emphasis on the 'active' infallibility of the *Ecclesia in credendo* was gradually replaced by an emphasis on the active role of the *Ecclesia docens*. It became common to say that the *Ecclesia discens* had only a 'passive' infallibility.

d) 19th Century

34. The 19th century was a decisive period for the doctrine of the *sensus fidei fidelium*. It saw, in the Catholic Church, partly in response to criticism from representatives of modern culture and from Christians of other traditions, and partly from an inner maturation, the rise of historical consciousness, a revival of interest in the Fathers of the Church and in medieval theologians, and a renewed exploration of the mystery of the Church. In this context, Catholic theologians such as Johann Adam Möhler (1796-1838), Giovanni Perrone (1794-1876), and John Henry Newman gave new attention to the *sensus fidei fidelium* as a *locus theologicus* in order to explain how the Holy Spirit maintains the whole Church in truth and to justify developments in the Church's doctrine. Theologians highlighted the active role of the whole Church, especially the contribution of the lay faithful, in preserving and transmitting the Church's faith; and the magisterium implicitly confirmed this insight in the process leading to the definition of the Immaculate Conception (1854).

35. To defend the Catholic faith against Rationalism, the Tübingen scholar, Johann Adam Möhler, sought to portray the Church as a living organism and to grasp the principles that governed the development of doctrine. In his view, it is the Holy Spirit who animates, guides, and unites

---

quod tenent omnes fideles tanquam de fide, necessario est verum et de fide; et similiter id quod docent omnes Episcopi tanquam ad fidem pertinens, necessario est verum et de fide' (p.73).

[32] *De controversiis* II, I, lib.2, cap.2: 'Concilium generale repraesentat Ecclesiam universam, et proinde consensum habet Ecclesiae universalis; quare si Ecclesia non potest errare, neque Concilium oecumenicum, legitimum et approbatum, potest errare' (p.28).

the faithful as a community in Christ, bringing about in them an ecclesial 'consciousness' of the faith (*Gemeingeist* or *Gesamtsinn*), something akin to a *Volksgeist* or national spirit.[33] This *sensus fidei*, which is the subjective dimension of Tradition, necessarily includes an objective element, the Church's teaching, for the Christian 'sense' of the faithful, which lives in their hearts and is virtually equivalent to Tradition, is never divorced from its content.[34]

36. John Henry Newman initially investigated the *sensus fidei fidelium* to resolve his difficulty concerning the development of doctrine. He was the first to publish an entire treatise on the latter topic, *An Essay on the Development of Christian Doctrine* (1845), and to spell out the characteristics of faithful development. To distinguish between true and false developments, he adopted Augustine's norm – the general consent of the whole Church, '*Securus iudicat orbis terrarum*' – but he saw that an infallible authority is necessary to maintain the Church in the truth.

37. Using insights from Möhler and Newman,[35] Perrone retrieved the patristic understanding of the *sensus fidelium* in order to respond to a widespread desire for a papal definition of Mary's Immaculate Conception; he found in the unanimous consent, or *conspiratio*, of the faithful and their pastors a warrant for the apostolic origin of this doctrine. He maintained that the most distinguished theologians attributed probative force to the *sensus fidelium*, and that the strength of one 'instrument of tradition' can make up for the deficit of another, e.g., 'the silence of the Fathers'.[36]

---

[33] J. A. Möhler, *Die Einheit in der Kirche oder das Prinzip des Katholizismus* [1825], ed. J. R. Geiselmann (Cologne and Olten: Jakob Hegner, 1957), 8ff., 50ff.

[34] J. A. Möhler, *Symbolik oder Darstellung der dogmatischen Gegensätze der Katholiken und Protestanten, nach ihren öffentlichen Bekenntnisschriften* [1832], ed. J.R. Geiselmann (Cologne and Olten: Jakob Hegner, 1958), §38. Against the Protestant principle of private interpretation, he reasserted the significance of the judgement of the whole Church.

[35] In 1847, Newman met Perrone and they discussed Newman's ideas about the development of doctrine. Newman used the notion of the *sensus ecclesiae* in this context. Cf. T. Lynch, ed., 'The Newman-Perrone Paper on Development', *Gregorianum* 16 (1935), pp.402-447, esp. ch.3, nn.2, 5.

[36] IOANNIS PERRONE, *De Immaculato B. V. Mariae Conceptu an Dogmatico Decreto definiri possit* (Romae, 1847), 139, 143-145. Perrone concluded that the Christian faithful would be 'deeply scandalised' if Mary's Immaculate Conception were 'even mildly questioned' (p.156). He found other instances in which the magisterium relied on the *sensus fidelium* for its doctrinal definitions, e.g. the doctrine that the souls of the just enjoy the beatific vision already prior to the resurrection of the dead (pp.147-148).

38. The influence of Perrone's research on Pope Pius IX's decision to proceed with the definition of the Immaculate Conception is evident from the fact that before he defined it the Pope asked the bishops of the world to report to him in writing regarding the devotion of their clergy and faithful people to the conception of the Immaculate Virgin.[37] In the apostolic constitution containing the definition, *Ineffabilis Deus* (1854), Pope Pius IX said that although he already knew the mind of the bishops on this matter, he had particularly asked the bishops to inform him of the piety and devotion of their faithful in this regard, and he concluded that 'Holy Scripture, venerable Tradition, the constant mind of the Church [*perpetuus Ecclesiae sensus*], the remarkable agreement of Catholic bishops and the faithful [*singularis catholicorum Antistitum ac fidelium conspiratio*], and the memorable Acts and Constitutions of our predecessors' all wonderfully illustrated and proclaimed the doctrine.[38] He thus used the language of Perrone's treatise to describe the combined testimony of the bishops and the faithful. Newman highlighted the word, *conspiratio*, and commented: 'the two, the Church teaching and the Church taught, are put together, as one twofold testimony, illustrating each other, and never to be divided'.[39]

39. When Newman later wrote *On Consulting the Faithful in Matters of Doctrine* (1859), it was to demonstrate that the faithful (as distinct from their pastors) have their own, active role to play in conserving and transmitting the faith. '[T]he tradition of the Apostles' is 'committed to the whole Church in its various constituents and functions per *modum unius*', but the bishops and the lay faithful bear witness to it in diverse ways. The tradition, he says, 'manifests itself variously at various times: sometimes by the mouth of the episcopacy, sometimes by the doctors, sometimes by the people, sometimes by liturgies, rites, ceremonies, and customs, by events, disputes, movements, and all those other phenomena which are comprised under the name of history'.[40] For Newman, 'there

---

[37] See POPE PIUS IX, Encyclical Letter, *Ubi primum* (1849), n.6.

[38] POPE PIUS IX, Apostolic Constitution, *Ineffabilis Deus* (1854).

[39] NEWMAN, *On Consulting the Faithful*, pp.70-71.

[40] NEWMAN, *On Consulting the Faithful*, p.63, cf. p.65. Newman usually distinguishes the 'pastors' and the 'faithful'. Sometimes he adds the 'doctors' (theologians) as a distinct class of witnesses, and he includes the lower clergy among the 'faithful' unless he specifies the 'lay faithful'.

is something in the *"pastorum et fidelium conspiratio"* which is not in the pastors alone'.[41] In this work, Newman quoted at length from the arguments proposed over a decade earlier by Giovanni Perrone in favour of the definition of the Immaculate Conception.[42]

40. The First Vatican Council's dogmatic constitution, *Pastor Aeternus*, in which the infallible magisterium of the pope was defined, by no means ignored the *sensus fidei fidelium*; on the contrary, it presupposed it. The original draft constitution, *Supremi Pastoris*, from which it developed, had a chapter on the infallibility of the Church (chapter nine).[43] When the order of business was changed in order to resolve the question of papal infallibility, however, discussion of that foundation was deferred and never taken up. In his *relatio* on the definition of papal infallibility, Bishop Vincent Gasser nevertheless explained that the special assistance given to the pope does not set him apart from the Church and does not exclude consultation and cooperation.[44] The definition of the Immaculate Conception was an example, he said, of a case 'so difficult that the Pope deems it necessary for his information to inquire from the bishops, as the ordinary means, what is the mind of the churches'.[45] In a phrase intended to exclude Gallicanism, *Pastor Aeternus* asserted that *ex cathedra* doctrinal definitions of the pope concerning faith and morals are irreformable 'of themselves and not from the consent of the Church [*ex sese non autem ex consensu ecclesiae*]',[46] but that does not make the *consensus Ecclesiae* superfluous. What it excludes is the theory that such a definition requires this consent, antecedent or consequent, as a condition for its authoritative status.[47] In response to the Modernist crisis, a decree from the Holy Office, *Lamentabili* (1907), confirmed the freedom of the *Ecclesia docens* vis-à-vis the *Ecclesia discens*. The decree

---

[41] NEWMAN, *On Consulting the Faithful*, p.104.

[42] NEWMAN, *On Consulting the Faithful*, pp.64-70; cf. above, §37.

[43] MANSI, III (51), 542-543. It asserts that the Church's infallibility extends to all revealed truth, in Scripture and in Tradition – i.e., to the Deposit of Faith – and to whatever is necessary for defending and preserving it, even though not revealed.

[44] MANSI, IV (52), 1213-14.

[45] Ibid., 1217. Gasser adds: 'sed talis casus non potest statui pro regula'.

[46] DH 3074. One of the 'Four Articles' of the Gallican position asserted that the Pope's judgement 'is not irreformable unless the consent of the Church be given to it'.

[47] See GASSER, in Mansi, 52, 1213-14.

censured a proposition that would allow the pastors to teach only what the faithful already believed.[48]

e) 20th Century

41. Catholic theologians in the 20th century explored the doctrine of the *sensus fidei fidelium* in the context of a theology of Tradition, a renewed ecclesiology, and a theology of the laity. They emphasised that 'the Church' is not identical with her pastors; that the whole Church, by the action of the Holy Spirit, is the subject or 'organ' of Tradition; and that lay people have an active role in the transmission of the apostolic faith. The magisterium endorsed these developments both in the consultation leading to the definition of the glorious Assumption of the Blessed Virgin Mary, and in the Second Vatican Council's retrieval and confirmation of the doctrine of the *sensus fidei*.

42. In 1946, following the pattern of his predecessor, Pope Pius XII sent an encyclical letter, *Deiparae Virginis Mariae*, to all the bishops of the world asking them to inform him 'about the devotion of your clergy and people (taking into account their faith and piety) toward the Assumption of the most Blessed Virgin Mary'. He thus reaffirmed the practice of consulting the faithful in advance of making a dogmatic definition, and, in the apostolic constitution, *Munificentissimus Deus* (1950), he reported the 'almost unanimous response' he had received.[49] Belief in Mary's Assumption was, indeed, 'thoroughly rooted in the minds of the faithful'.[50] Pope Pius XII referred to 'the concordant teaching of the Church's ordinary doctrinal authority and the concordant faith of the Christian people', and said, with regard now to belief in Mary's Assumption, as Pope Pius IX had said with regard to belief in her Immaculate Conception, that there was a '*singularis catholicorum Antistitum et fidelium conspiratio*'. He added that the *conspiratio* showed 'in an entirely certain and infallible way' that Mary's Assumption was 'a truth revealed by God and contained in that divine deposit which Christ delivered to his Spouse to be guarded

---

[48] The condemned proposition reads: 'The "Church learning" and the "Church teaching" collaborate in such a way in defining truths that it only remains for the "Church teaching" to sanction the opinions of the "Church learning"' (DH 3406).

[49] POPE PIUS XII, Apostolic Constitution, *Munificentissimus Deus*, n.12.

[50] *Munificentissimus Deus,* n.41.

faithfully and to be taught infallibly'.[51] In both cases, then, the papal definitions confirmed and celebrated the deeply-held beliefs of the faithful.

43. Yves M.-J. Congar (1904-1995) contributed significantly to the development of the doctrine of the *sensus fidei fidelis* and the *sensus fidei fidelium*. In *Jalons pour une Théologie du Laïcat* (orig. 1953), he explored this doctrine in terms of the participation of the laity in the Church's prophetical function. Congar was acquainted with Newman's work and adopted the same scheme (i.e. the threefold office of the Church, and the *sensus fidelium* as an expression of the prophetic office) without, however, tracing it directly to Newman.[52] He described the *sensus fidelium* as a gift of the Holy Spirit 'given to the hierarchy and the whole body of the faithful together', and he distinguished the objective reality of faith (which constitutes the tradition) from the subjective aspect, the grace of faith.[53] Where earlier authors had underlined the distinction between the *Ecclesia docens* and the *Ecclesia discens*, Congar was concerned to show their organic unity. 'The Church loving and believing, that is, the body of the faithful, is infallible in the living possession of the faith, not in a particular act or judgement', he wrote.[54] The teaching of the hierarchy is at the service of communion.

44. In many ways, the Second Vatican Council's teaching reflects Congar's contribution. Chapter one of *Lumen Gentium*, on 'The Mystery of the Church', teaches that the Holy Spirit 'dwells in the Church and in the hearts of the faithful, as in a temple'. 'Guiding the Church in the way of all truth (cf. *Jn* 16:13) and unifying her in communion and in the works of ministry, he bestows upon her varied hierarchic and charismatic gifts, and in this way directs her; and he adorns her with his fruits (cf. *Ep* 4:11-12; *1 Co* 12:4; *Gal* 5:22)'.[55] Chapter two then continues to deal with the Church as a whole, as the 'People of God', prior to distinctions between lay and ordained. The article (*LG* 12) which mentions the *sensus fidei* teaches that, having 'an anointing that comes from the holy one (cf. *1 Jn* 2:20, 27)', the 'whole body of the faithful ... cannot err in matters of belief'. The 'Spirit

---

[51] *Munificentissimus Deus*, n.12.

[52] See CONGAR, *Jalons pour une Théologie du Laïcat*, chapter 6. The scheme is found in the Preface of the third edition of Newman's *Via Media* (1877).

[53] CONGAR, *Jalons pour une Théologie du Laïcat*, p.398; ET, *Lay People in the Church*, 288.

[54] *Jalons pour une Théologie du Laïcat*, p.399; ET, *Lay People in the Church*, 289.

[55] LG 4.

of truth' arouses and sustains a 'supernatural appreciation of the faith [*supernaturali sensu fidei*]', shown when 'the whole people, ... "from the bishops to the last of the faithful" ... manifest a universal consent in matters of faith and morals'. By means of the *sensus fidei*, 'the People of God, guided by the sacred teaching authority (magisterium), and obeying it, receives not the mere word of men, but truly the word of God (cf. *1 Th* 2:13)'. According to this description, the *sensus fidei* is an active capacity or sensibility by which they are able to receive and understand the 'faith once for all delivered to the saints (cf. Jude 3)'. Indeed, by means of it, the people not only 'unfailingly adheres to this faith', but also 'penetrates it more deeply with right judgement, and applies it more fully in daily life'. It is the means by which the people shares in 'Christ's prophetic office'.[56]

45. *Lumen Gentium* subsequently describes, in chapters three and four, respectively, how Christ exercises his prophetic office not only through the Church's pastors, but also through the lay faithful. It teaches that, 'until the full manifestation of his glory', the Lord fulfils this office 'not only by the hierarchy who teach in his name and by his power, but also by the laity'. With regard to the latter, it continues: 'He accordingly both establishes them as witnesses and provides them with the appreciation of the faith and the grace of the word [*sensu fidei et gratia verbi instruit*] (cf. *Ac* 2:17-18; *Rv* 19:10) so that the power of the Gospel may shine out in daily family and social life.' Strengthened by the sacraments, 'the laity become powerful heralds of the faith in things to be hoped for (cf. *Heb* 11:1)'; 'the laity can, and must, do valuable work for the evangelisation of the world'.[57] Here, the *sensus fidei* is presented as Christ's gift to the faithful, and once again is described as an active capacity by which the faithful are able to understand, live and proclaim the truths of divine revelation. It is the basis for their work of evangelisation.

46. The *sensus fidei* is also evoked in the council's teaching on the development of doctrine, in the context of the transmission of the apostolic faith. *Dei Verbum* says that the apostolic Tradition 'makes progress in the

---

[56] LG 12. In several other places, the council refers to the 'sense' of believers or of the Church in a way analogous to the *sensus fidei* of LG 12. It refers to the *sensus Ecclesiae* (DV 23), *sensus apostolicus* (AA 25), *sensus catholicus* (AA 30), *sensus Christi et Ecclesiae* and *sensus communionis cum Ecclesia* (AG 19), *sensus christianus fidelium* (GS 52), and to an *integer christianus sensus* (GS 62).

[57] LG 35.

Church, with the help of the Holy Spirit'. 'There is a growth in insight into the realities and words that are being passed on', and the council identifies three ways in which this happens: 'through the contemplation and study of believers who ponder these things in their hearts (cf. *Lk* 2:19 and 51)'; 'from the intimate sense of spiritual realities which they experience [*ex intima spiritualium rerum quam experiuntur intelligentia*]'; and 'from the preaching of those [the bishops] who have received ... the sure charism of truth'.[58] Although this passage does not name the *sensus fidei*, the contemplation, study, and experience of believers to which it refers are all clearly associated with the *sensus fidei*, and most commentators agree that the council fathers were consciously invoking Newman's theory of the development of doctrine. When this text is read in light of the description of the *sensus fidei* in *Lumen Gentium* 12 as a supernatural appreciation of the faith, aroused by the Holy Spirit, by which people guided by their pastors adhere unfailingly to the faith, it is readily seen to express the same idea. When referring to 'the remarkable harmony' that should exist between the bishops and the faithful in the practice and profession of the faith handed on by the apostles, *Dei Verbum* actually uses the very expression found in the definitions of both Marian dogmas, '*singularis fiat Antistitum et fidelium conspiratio*'.[59]

47. Since the council, the magisterium has reiterated key points from the council's teaching on the *sensus fidei*,[60] and also addressed a new issue, namely, the importance of not presuming that public opinion inside (or outside) the Church is necessarily the same thing as the *sensus fidei* (*fidelium*). In the post-synodal apostolic exhortation, *Familiaris Consortio* (1981), Pope John Paul II considered the question as to how the 'supernatural sense of faith' may be related to the 'consensus of the faithful' and to majority opinion as determined by sociological and statistical research. The *sensus fidei*, he wrote, 'does not consist solely or necessarily in the consensus of the faithful'. It is the task of the Church's

---

[58] DV 8.

[59] DV 10; cf. *Ineffabilis Deus*, n.18, and *Munificentissimus Deus*, n.12.

[60] See, e.g., POPE JOHN PAUL II's teaching in his Apostolic Exhortation, *Christifideles Laici* (1988), that all the faithful share in Christ's threefold office, and his reference to the laity being 'sharers in the appreciation of the Church's supernatural faith (*sensum fidei supernaturalis Ecclesiae*) that "cannot err in matters of belief" [LG 12]' (n.14); also, with reference to the teaching of LG 12, 35, and DV 8, the declaration of the Congregation for the Doctrine of the Faith (CDF), *Mysterium Ecclesiae* (1973), n.2.

pastors to 'promote the sense of the faith in all the faithful, examine and authoritatively judge the genuineness of its expressions, and educate the faithful in an ever more mature evangelical discernment'.[61]

---

[61] POPE JOHN PAUL II, Apostolic Exhortation, *Familiaris Consortio* (1981), n.5. In its Instruction on the Ecclesial Vocation of the Theologian, *Donum Veritatis* (1990), the CDF cautioned against identifying 'the opinion of a large number of Christians' with the *sensus fidei*: the *sensus fidei* is 'a property of theological faith' and a gift of God which enables a Christian 'to adhere personally to the Truth', so that what he or she believes is what the Church believes. Since not all the opinions held by believers spring from faith, and since many people are swayed by public opinion, it is necessary to emphasise, as the council did, the 'indissoluble bond between the *"sensus fidei"* and the guidance of God's People by the Magisterium of the Pastors' (n.35).

CHAPTER TWO

THE SENSUS FIDEI FIDELIS IN THE PERSONAL LIFE OF THE BELIEVER

48. This second chapter concentrates on the nature of the *sensus fidei fidelis*. It utilises, in particular, the framework of arguments and categories offered by classical theology in order to reflect how faith is operative in individual believers. Although the Biblical vision of faith is larger, the classical understanding highlights an essential aspect: the adherence of the intellect, through love, to revealed truth. This conceptualisation of faith serves still today to clarify the understanding of the *sensus fidei fidelis*. In these terms, the chapter also considers some manifestations of the *sensus fidei fidelis* in the personal lives of believers, it being clear that the personal and ecclesial aspects of the *sensus fidei* are inseparable.

1. THE SENSUS FIDEI AS AN INSTINCT OF FAITH

49. The *sensus fidei fidelis* is a sort of spiritual instinct that enables the believer to judge spontaneously whether a particular teaching or practice is or is not in conformity with the Gospel and with apostolic faith. It is intrinsically linked to the virtue of faith itself; it flows from, and is a property of, faith.[62] It is compared to an instinct because it is not primarily the result of rational deliberation, but rather a form of spontaneous and natural knowledge, a sort of perception (*aisthesis*).

50. The *sensus fidei fidelis* arises, first and foremost, from the connaturality that the virtue of faith establishes between the believing subject and the authentic object of faith, namely the truth of God revealed in Christ Jesus. Generally speaking, connaturality refers to a situation in which an entity A has a relationship with another entity B so intimate that A shares in the natural dispositions of B as if they were its own. Connaturality

---

[62] The *sensus fidei fidelis* presupposes in the believer the virtue of faith. In fact, it is the lived experience of faith which enables the believer to discern whether a doctrine belongs to the deposit of faith or not. It is therefore only rather broadly and derivatively that the discernment necessary for the initial act of faith can be attributed to the *sensus fidei fidelis*.

permits a particular and profound form of knowledge. For example, to the extent that one friend is united to another, he or she becomes capable of judging spontaneously what suits the other because he or she shares the very inclinations of the other and so understands by connaturality what is good or bad for the other. This is a knowledge, in other words, of a different order than objective knowledge, which proceeds by way of conceptualisation and reasoning. It is a knowledge by empathy, or a knowledge of the heart.

51. Every virtue connaturalises its subject, in other words the one who possesses it, to its object, that is, to a certain type of action. What is meant by virtue here is the stable disposition (or *habitus*) of a person to behave in a certain way either intellectually or morally. Virtue is a kind of 'second nature', by which the human person constructs himself or herself by actualising freely and in accord with right reason the dynamisms inscribed in human nature. It thereby gives a definite, stable orientation to the activity of the natural faculties; it directs the latter to behaviours which the virtuous person henceforth accomplishes 'naturally', with 'ease, self-mastery and joy'.[63]

52. Every virtue has a double effect: first, it naturally inclines the person who possesses it towards an object (a certain kind of action), and second, it spontaneously distances him or her from whatever is contrary to that object. For example, a person who has developed the virtue of chastity possesses a sort of 'sixth sense', 'a kind of spiritual instinct',[64] which enables him or her to discern the right way to behave even in the most complex situations, spontaneously perceiving what it is appropriate to do and what to avoid. A chaste person thereby instinctively adopts the right attitude, where the conceptual reasoning of the moralist might lead to perplexity and indecision.[65]

53. The *sensus fidei* is the form that the instinct which accompanies every virtue takes in the case of the virtue of faith. 'Just as, by the habits of the other virtues, one sees what is becoming in respect of that habit, so, by the habit of faith, the human mind is directed to assent to such things as

---

[63] CCC 1804.

[64] VATICAN II, PC 12.

[65] Cf. THOMAS AQUINAS, *Summa theologiae*, IIa-IIae, q.45, a.2.

are becoming to a right faith, and not to assent to others.'[66] Faith, as a theological virtue, enables the believer to participate in the knowledge that God has of himself and of all things. In the believer, it takes the form of a 'second nature'.[67] By means of grace and the theological virtues, believers become 'participants of the divine nature' (*2 Pet* 1:4), and are in a way connaturalised to God. As a result, they react spontaneously on the basis of that participated divine nature, in the same way that living beings react instinctively to what does or does not suit their nature.

54. Unlike theology, which can be described as *scientia fidei*, the *sensus fidei fidelis* is not a reflective knowledge of the mysteries of faith which deploys concepts and uses rational procedures to reach its conclusions. As its name (*sensus*) indicates, it is akin rather to a natural, immediate and spontaneous reaction, and comparable to a vital instinct or a sort of 'flair' by which the believer clings spontaneously to what conforms to the truth of faith and shuns what is contrary to it.[68]

55. The *sensus fidei fidelis* is infallible in itself with regard to its object: the true faith.[69] However, in the actual mental universe of the believer, the correct intuitions of the *sensus fidei* can be mixed up with various purely human opinions, or even with errors linked to the narrow confines of a particular cultural context.[70] 'Although theological faith as such cannot err, the believer can still have erroneous opinions since all his thoughts do not spring from faith. Not all the ideas which circulate among the People of God are compatible with the faith.'[71]

---

[66] THOMAS AQUINAS, *Summa theologiae*, IIa-IIae, q.1, a.4, ad 3. Cf. IIa-IIae, q.2, a.3, ad 2.

[67] Cf. THOMAS AQUINAS, *Scriptum*, III, d.23, q.3, a.3, qla 2, ad 2: 'Habitus fidei cum non rationi innitatur, inclinat per modum naturae, sicut et habitus moralium virtutum, et sicut habitus principiorum; et ideo quamdiu manet, nihil contra fidem credit.'

[68] Cf. J. A. MÖHLER, *Symbolik*, §38: 'Der göttliche Geist, welchem die Leitung und Belebung der Kirche anvertraut ist, wird in seiner Vereinigung mit dem menschlichen ein eigenthümlich christlicher Tact, ein tiefes, sicher führendes Gefühl, das, wie er in der Wahrheit steht, auch aller Wahrheit entgegenleitet.'

[69] Because of its immediate relationship to its object, instinct does not err. In itself, it is infallible. However, animal instinct is infallible only within the context of a determined environment. When the context changes, animal instinct can show itself to be maladjusted. Spiritual instinct, on the other hand, has more scope and subtlety.

[70] Cf. THOMAS AQUINAS, *Summa theologiae*, IIa-IIae, q.1, a.3, ad 3.

[71] CDF, *Donum Veritatis*, n.35.

56. The *sensus fidei fidelis* flows from the theological virtue of faith. That virtue is an interior disposition, prompted by love, to adhere without reserve to the whole truth revealed by God as soon as it is perceived as such. Faith does not therefore necessarily imply an explicit knowledge of the whole of revealed truth.[72] It follows that a certain type of *sensus fidei* can exist in 'the baptised who are honoured by the name of Christian, but who do not however profess the Catholic faith in its entirety'.[73] The Catholic Church therefore needs to be attentive to what the Spirit may be saying to her by means of believers in the churches and ecclesial communities not fully in communion with her.

57. Since it is a property of the theological virtue of faith, the *sensus fidei fidelis* develops in proportion to the development of the virtue of faith. The more the virtue of faith takes root in the heart and spirit of believers and informs their daily life, the more the *sensus fidei fidelis* develops and strengthens in them. Now, since faith, understood as a form of knowledge, is based on love, charity is needed in order to animate it and to inform it, so as to make it a living and lived faith (*fides formata*). Thus, the intensifying of faith within the believer particularly depends on the growth within him or her of charity, and the *sensus fidei fidelis* is therefore proportional to the holiness of one's life. St Paul teaches that 'God's love has been poured into our hearts through the Holy Spirit that has been given to us' (*Rm* 5:5), and it follows that the development of the *sensus fidei* in the spirit of the believer is particularly due to the action of the Holy Spirit. As the Spirit of love, who instils love in human hearts, the Holy Spirit opens to believers the possibility of a deeper and more intimate knowledge of Christ the Truth, on the basis of a union of charity: 'Showing the truth is a property of the Holy Spirit, because it is love which brings about the revelation of secrets'.[74]

58. Charity enables the flourishing in believers of the gifts of the Holy Spirit, who leads them to a higher understanding of the things of faith 'in all spiritual wisdom and understanding' (*Col* 1:9).[75] In fact, the

---

[72] Cf. THOMAS AQUINAS, *Summa theologiae*, IIa-IIae, q.2, a.5-8.

[73] LG 15.

[74] THOMAS AQUINAS, *Expositio super Ioannis evangelium*, c.14, lect.4 (Marietti, n.1916).

[75] Cf. ITC, *Theology Today*, §§91-92.

theological virtues attain their full measure in the believer's life only when the believer allows the Holy Spirit to guide him or her (cf. *Rm* 8:14). The gifts of the Spirit are precisely the gratuitous and infused interior dispositions which serve as a basis for the activity of the Spirit in the life of the believer. By means of these gifts of the Spirit, especially the gifts of understanding and knowledge, believers are made capable of understanding intimately the 'spiritual realities which they experience',[76] and rejecting any interpretation contrary to the faith.

59. There is a vital interaction in each believer between the *sensus fidei* and the living of faith in the various contexts of his or her personal life. On one hand, the *sensus fidei* enlightens and guides the way in which the believer puts his or her faith into practice. On the other hand, by keeping the commandments and putting faith into practice, the believer gains a deeper understanding of faith: 'those who do what is true come to the light, so that it may be clearly seen that their deeds have been done in God' (*Jn* 3:21). Putting faith into practice in the concrete reality of the existential situations in which he or she is placed by family, professional and cultural relations enriches the personal experience of the believer. It enables him or her to see more precisely the value and the limits of a given doctrine, and to propose ways of refining its formulation. That is why those who teach in the name of the Church should give full attention to the experience of believers, especially lay people, who strive to put the Church's teaching into practice in the areas of their own specific experience and competence.

2. MANIFESTATIONS OF THE SENSUS FIDEI IN THE PERSONAL LIFE OF BELIEVERS

60. Three principal manifestations of the *sensus fidei fidelis* in the personal life of the believer can be highlighted. The *sensus fidei fidelis* enables individual believers: 1) to discern whether or not a particular teaching or practice that they actually encounter in the Church is coherent with the true faith by which they live in the communion of the Church (see below,

---

[76] DV 8. In the theology of the gifts of the Spirit that St Thomas developed, it is particularly the gift of knowledge that perfects the *sensus fidei fidelis* as an aptitude to discern what is to be believed. Cf. THOMAS AQUINAS, *Summa theologiae*, IIa-IIae, q.9, a.1 co. et ad 2.

§§61-63); 2) to distinguish in what is preached between the essential
and the secondary (§64); and 3) to determine and put into practice the
witness to Jesus Christ that they should give in the particular historical
and cultural context in which they live (§65).

61. 'Beloved, do not believe every spirit, but test the spirits to see whether
they are from God ; for many false prophets have gone out into the world'
(*1 Jn* 4:1). The *sensus fidei fidelis* confers on the believer the capacity to
discern whether or not a teaching or practice is coherent with the true faith
by which he or she already lives. If individual believers perceive or 'sense'
that coherence, they spontaneously give their interior adherence to those
teachings or engage personally in the practices, whether it is a matter of
truths already explicitly taught or of truths not yet explicitly taught.

62. The *sensus fidei fidelis* also enables individual believers to perceive
any disharmony, incoherence, or contradiction between a teaching or
practice and the authentic Christian faith by which they live. They react
as a music lover does to false notes in the performance of a piece of
music. In such cases, believers interiorly resist the teachings or practices
concerned and do not accept them or participate in them. 'The *habitus* of
faith possesses a capacity whereby, thanks to it, the believer is prevented
from giving assent to what is contrary to the faith, just as chastity gives
protection with regard to whatever is contrary to chastity.'[77]

63. Alerted by their *sensus fidei*, individual believers may deny assent even
to the teaching of legitimate pastors if they do not recognise in that teaching
the voice of Christ, the Good Shepherd. 'The sheep follow [the Good
Shepherd] because they know his voice. They will not follow a stranger,
but they will run away from him because they do not know the voice of
strangers' (*Jn* 10:4-5). For St Thomas, a believer, even without theological
competence, can and even must resist, by virtue of the *sensus fidei*, his or
her bishop if the latter preaches heterodoxy.[78] In such a case, the believer

[77] Thomas Aquinas, *Quaestiones disputatae de veritate*, q.14, a.10, ad 10; cf. *Scriptum*, III,
d.25, q.2, a.1, qla 2, ad 3.

[78] Thomas Aquinas, *Scriptum*, III, d.25, q.2, a.1, qla 4, ad 3: '[The believer] must not give
assent to a prelate who preaches against the faith…. The subordinate is not totally excused
by his ignorance. In fact, the habitus of faith inclines him against such preaching because
that habitus necessarily teaches whatever leads to salvation. Also, because one must not
give credence too easily to every spirit, one should not give assent to strange preaching but

does not treat himself or herself as the ultimate criterion of the truth of faith, but rather, faced with materially 'authorised' preaching which he or she finds troubling, without being able to explain exactly why, defers assent and appeals interiorly to the superior authority of the universal Church.[79]

64. The *sensus fidei fidelis* also enables the believer to distinguish in what is preached between what is essential for an authentic Catholic faith and what, without being formally against the faith, is only accidental or even indifferent with regard to the core of the faith. For example, by virtue of their *sensus fidei,* individual believers may relativise certain particular forms of Marian devotion precisely out of adherence to an authentic cult of the Virgin Mary. They might also distance themselves from preaching which unduly mixes together Christian faith and partisan political choices. By keeping the spirit of the believer focused in this way on what is essential to the faith, the *sensus fidei fidelis* guarantees an authentic Christian liberty (cf. *Col* 2:16-23), and contributes to a purification of faith.

65. Thanks to the *sensus fidei fidelis* and sustained by the supernatural prudence that the Spirit confers, the believer is able to sense, in new historical and cultural contexts, what might be the most appropriate ways in which to give an authentic witness to the truth of Jesus Christ, and moreover to act accordingly. The *sensus fidei fidelis* thus acquires a prospective dimension to the extent that, on the basis of the faith already lived, it enables the believer to anticipate a development or an explanation of Christian practice. Because of the reciprocal link between the practice of the faith and the understanding of its content, the *sensus fidei fidelis* contributes in this way to the emergence and illumination of aspects of the Catholic faith that were previously implicit; and because of the reciprocal link between the *sensus fidei* of the individual believer and the *sensus fidei* of the Church as such, that is the *sensus fidei fidelium*, such developments are never purely private, but always ecclesial. The faithful are always in relationship with one another, and with the magisterium and theologians, in the communion of the Church.

---

should seek further information or simply entrust oneself to God without seeking to venture into the secrets of God beyond one's capacities.'

[79] Cf. Thomas Aquinas, *Scriptum*, III, d.25, q.2, a.1, qla 2, ad 3; *Quaestiones disputatae de veritate*, q.14, a.11, ad 2.

CHAPTER THREE

THE SENSUS FIDEI FIDELIUM IN THE LIFE OF THE CHURCH

66. As the faith of the individual believer participates in the faith of the Church as a believing subject, so the *sensus fidei* (*fidelis*) of individual believers cannot be separated from the *sensus fidei* (*fidelium*) or '*sensus Ecclesiae*'[80] of the Church herself, endowed and sustained by the Holy Spirit,[81] and the *consensus fidelium* constitutes a sure criterion for recognising a particular teaching or practice as in accord with the apostolic Tradition.[82] The present chapter, therefore, turns to consider various aspects of the *sensus fidei fidelium*. It reflects, first of all, on the role of the latter in the development of Christian doctrine and practice; then on two relationships of great importance for the life and health of the Church, namely the relationship between the *sensus fidei* and the magisterium, and the relationship between the *sensus fidei* and theology; then, finally, on some ecumenical aspects of the *sensus fidei*.

1. THE SENSUS FIDEI AND THE DEVELOPMENT OF CHRISTIAN DOCTRINE AND PRACTICE

67. The whole Church, laity and hierarchy together, bears responsibility for and mediates in history the revelation which is contained in the holy Scriptures and in the living apostolic Tradition. The Second Vatican Council stated that the latter form 'a single sacred deposit of the word of God' which is 'entrusted to the Church', that is, 'the entire holy people, united to its pastors'.[83] The council clearly taught that the faithful are not merely passive recipients of what the hierarchy teaches and theologians explain;

---

[80] See above, §30.

[81] See CONGAR, *La Tradition et les traditions*, II, pp.81-101, on 'L'"Ecclesia", sujet de la Tradition', and pp.101-108, on 'Le Saint-Esprit, Sujet transcendant de la Tradition'; ET, *Tradition and Traditions*, pp.314-338, on 'The "Ecclesia" as the Subject of Tradition', and pp.338-346, on 'The Holy Spirit, the Transcendent Subject of Tradition'.

[82] See above, §3.

[83] DV 10 (amended translation).

rather, they are living and active subjects within the Church. In this context, it underscored the vital role played by all believers in the articulation and development of the faith: 'the Tradition that comes from the apostles makes progress in the Church, with the help of the Holy Spirit'.[84]

a) Retrospective and prospective aspects of the sensus fidei

68. In order to understand how it functions and manifests itself in the life of the Church, the *sensus fidei* needs to be viewed within the context of history, a history in which the Holy Spirit makes each day a day to hear the voice of the Lord afresh (cf. *Heb* 3:7-15). The Good News of the life, death and resurrection of Jesus Christ is transmitted to the Church as a whole through the living apostolic Tradition, of which the Scriptures are the authoritative written witness. Hence, by the grace of the Holy Spirit, who reminds the Church of all that Jesus said and did (cf. *Jn* 14:26), believers rely on the Scriptures and on the continuing apostolic Tradition in their life of faith and in the exercise of the *sensus fidei*.

69. However, faith and the *sensus fidei* are not only anchored in the past; they are also orientated towards the future. The communion of believers is a historical reality: 'built upon the foundation of the apostles and the prophets, with Christ Jesus himself as the cornerstone', it 'grows into a holy temple in the Lord' (*Ep* 2:20-21), in the power of the Holy Spirit, who guides the Church 'into all the truth' and declares to believers already now 'the things that are to come' (*Jn* 16:13), so that, especially in the Eucharist, the Church anticipates the return of the Lord and the coming of his kingdom (cf. *1 Co* 11:26).

70. As she awaits the return of her Lord, the Church and her members are constantly confronted with new circumstances, with the progress of knowledge and culture, and with the challenges of human history, and they have to read the signs of the times, 'to interpret them in the light of the divine Word', and to discern how they may enable revealed truth itself to be 'more deeply penetrated, better understood and more deeply presented'.[85] In this process, the *sensus fidei fidelium* has an essential role to play. It is not only reactive but also proactive and interactive, as the Church and

---

[84] DV 8; cf. also, LG 12, 37; AA 2, 3; GS 43.

[85] GS 44 (amended translation).

all of its members make their pilgrim way in history. The *sensus fidei* is therefore not only retrospective but also prospective, and, though less familiar, the prospective and proactive aspects of the *sensus fidei* are highly important. The *sensus fidei* gives an intuition as to the right way forward amid the uncertainties and ambiguities of history, and a capacity to listen discerningly to what human culture and the progress of the sciences are saying. It animates the life of faith and guides authentic Christian action.

71. It can take a long time before this process of discernment comes to a conclusion. In the face of new circumstances, the faithful at large, pastors and theologians all have their respective roles to play, and patience and respect are needed in their mutual interactions if the *sensus fidei* is to be clarified and a true *consensus fidelium*, a *conspiratio pastorum et fidelium*, is to be achieved.

b) The contribution of the laity to the sensus fidelium

72. From the beginning of Christianity, all the faithful played an active role in the development of Christian belief. The whole community bore witness to the apostolic faith, and history shows that, when decisions about the faith needed to be taken, the witness of the laity was taken into consideration by the pastors. As has been seen in the historical survey above,[86] there is evidence that the laity played a major role in the coming into existence of various doctrinal definitions. Sometimes the people of God, and in particular the laity, intuitively felt in which direction the development of doctrine would go, even when theologians and bishops were divided on the issue. Sometimes there was a clear *conspiratio pastorum et fidelium.* Sometimes, when the Church came to a definition, the *Ecclesia docens* had clearly 'consulted' the faithful, and it pointed to the *consensus fidelium* as one of the arguments which legitimated the definition.

73. What is less well known, and generally receives less attention, is the role played by the laity with regard to the development of the moral teaching of the Church. It is therefore important to reflect also on the function played by the laity in discerning the Christian understanding of appropriate human behaviour in accordance with the Gospel. In certain areas, the teaching of the Church has developed as a result of lay people

---

[86] See above, Chapter One, part 2.

discovering the imperatives arising from new situations. The reflection of theologians, and then the judgement of the episcopal magisterium, was based on the Christian experience already clarified by the faithful intuition of lay people. Some examples might illustrate the role of the *sensus fidelium* in the development of moral doctrine:

i) Between canon 20 of the Council of Elvira (c. 306 AD), which forbade clerics and lay people to receive interest, and the response, *Non esse inquietandos*, of Pope Pius VIII to the bishop of Rennes (1830),[87] there is a clear development of teaching, due to both the emergence of a new awareness among lay people involved in business as well as new reflection on the part of theologians with regard to the nature of money.

ii) The openness of the Church towards social problems, especially manifest in Pope Leo XIII's Encyclical Letter, *Rerum Novarum* (1896), was the fruit of a slow preparation in which lay 'social pioneers', activists as well as thinkers, played a major role.

iii) The striking albeit homogeneous development from the condemnation of 'liberal' theses in part 10 of the Syllabus of Errors (1864) of Pope Pius IX to the declaration on religious liberty, *Dignitatis Humanae* (1965), of Vatican II would not have been possible without the commitment of many Christians in the struggle for human rights.

The difficulty of discerning the authentic *sensus fidelium* in cases such as those above particularly indicates the need to identify dispositions required for authentic participation in the *sensus fidei,* dispositions which may serve, in turn, as criteria for discerning the authentic *sensus fidei.*[88]

2. THE SENSUS FIDEI AND THE MAGISTERIUM

a) The magisterium listens to the sensus fidelium

74. In matters of faith the baptised cannot be passive. They have received the Spirit and are endowed as members of the body of the Lord with gifts and charisms 'for the renewal and building up of the Church',[89] so the magisterium has to be attentive to the *sensus fidelium*, the living voice of

---

[87] Cf. DH 2722-2724.

[88] See below, Chapter Four.

[89] LG 12.

the people of God. Not only do they have the right to be heard, but their reaction to what is proposed as belonging to the faith of the Apostles must be taken very seriously, because it is by the Church as a whole that the apostolic faith is borne in the power of the Spirit. The magisterium does not have sole responsibility for it. The magisterium should therefore refer to the sense of faith of the Church as a whole. The *sensus fidelium* can be an important factor in the development of doctrine, and it follows that the magisterium needs means by which to consult the faithful.

75. The connection between the *sensus fidelium* and the magisterium is particularly to be found in the liturgy. The faithful are baptised into a royal priesthood, exercised principally in the Eucharist,[90] and the bishops are the 'high priests' who preside at the Eucharist,[91] regularly exercising there their teaching office, also. The Eucharist is the source and summit of the life of the Church;[92] it is there especially that the faithful and their pastors interact, as one body for one purpose, namely to give praise and glory to God. The Eucharist shapes and forms the *sensus fidelium* and contributes greatly to the formulation and refinement of verbal expressions of the faith, because it is there that the teaching of bishops and councils is ultimately 'received' by the faithful. From early Christian times, the Eucharist underpinned the formulation of the Church's doctrine because there most of all was the mystery of faith encountered and celebrated, and the bishops who presided at the Eucharist of their local churches among their faithful people were those who gathered in councils to determine how best to express the faith in words and formulas: *lex orandi, lex credendi*.[93]

b) The magisterium nurtures, discerns and judges the sensus fidelium

76. The magisterium of those 'who have received, along with their right of succession in the episcopate, the sure charism of truth'[94] is a ministry of truth exercised in and for the Church, all of whose members have

---

[90] Cf. LG 10, 34.

[91] Cf. LG 21, 26; SC 41.

[92] Cf. SC 10; LG 11.

[93] CCC 1124. Cf. IRENAEUS, *Adv.Haer.*, IV, 18, 5 (Sources chrétiennes, vol.100, p.610): 'Our way of thinking is attuned to the Eucharist, and the Eucharist in turn confirms our way of thinking' (see also CCC, n.1327).

[94] DV 8.

been anointed by the Spirit of truth (*Jn* 14:17; 15:26; 16:13; *1 Jn* 2:20, 27), and endowed with the *sensus fidei*, an instinct for the truth of the Gospel. Being responsible for ensuring the fidelity of the Church as a whole to the word of God, and for keeping the people of God faithful to the Gospel, the magisterium is responsible for nurturing and educating the *sensus fidelium*. Of course, those who exercise the magisterium, namely the pope and the bishops, are themselves, first of all, baptised members of the people of God, who participate by that very fact in the *sensus fidelium*.

77. The magisterium also judges with authority whether opinions which are present among the people of God, and which may seem to be the *sensus fidelium*, actually correspond to the truth of the Tradition received from the Apostles. As Newman said: 'the gift of discerning, discriminating, defining, promulgating, and enforcing any portion of that tradition resides solely in the *Ecclesia docens*'.[95] Thus, judgement regarding the authenticity of the *sensus fidelium* belongs ultimately not to the faithful themselves nor to theology but to the magisterium. Nevertheless, as already emphasised, the faith which it serves is the faith of the Church, which lives in all of the faithful, so it is always within the communion life of the Church that the magisterium exercises its essential ministry of oversight.

c) Reception

78. 'Reception' may be described as a process by which, guided by the Spirit, the people of God recognises intuitions or insights and integrates them into the patterns and structures of its life and worship, accepting a new witness to the truth and corresponding forms of its expression, because it perceives them to be in accord with the apostolic Tradition. The process of reception is fundamental for the life and health of the Church as a pilgrim people journeying in history towards the fulness of God's Kingdom.

79. All of the gifts of the Spirit, and in a special way the gift of primacy in the Church, are given so as to foster the unity of the Church in faith and communion,[96] and the reception of magisterial teaching by the faithful is itself prompted by the Spirit, as the faithful, by means of the *sensus fidei* that they possess, recognise the truth of what is taught and cling to it. As

---

[95] NEWMAN, *On Consulting the Faithful*, p.63.

[96] Cf. VATICAN I, *Pastor Aeternus*, DH 3051.

was explained above, the teaching of Vatican I that infallible definitions of the pope are irreformable 'of themselves and not from the consent of the Church [*ex sese non autem ex consensu ecclesiae*]'[97] does not mean that the pope is cut off from the Church or that his teaching is independent of the faith of the Church.[98] The fact that prior to the infallible definitions both of the Immaculate Conception of the Blessed Virgin Mary and of her bodily Assumption into heaven an extensive consultation of the faithful was carried out at the express wish of the pope at that time amply proves the point.[99] What is meant, rather, is that such teaching of the pope, and by extension all teaching of the pope and of the bishops, is authoritative in itself because of the gift of the Holy Spirit, the *charisma veritatis certum*, that they possess.

80. There are occasions, however, when the reception of magisterial teaching by the faithful meets with difficulty and resistance, and appropriate action on both sides is required in such situations. The faithful must reflect on the teaching that has been given, making every effort to understand and accept it. Resistance, as a matter of principle, to the teaching of the magisterium is incompatible with the authentic *sensus fidei*. The magisterium must likewise reflect on the teaching that has been given and consider whether it needs clarification or reformulation in order to communicate more effectively the essential message. These mutual efforts in times of difficulty themselves express the communion that is essential to the life of the Church, and likewise a yearning for the grace of the Spirit who guides the Church 'into all the truth' (*Jn* 16:13).

3. THE SENSUS FIDEI AND THEOLOGY

81. As a service towards the understanding of faith, theology endeavours, amid the *conspiratio* of all the charisms and functions in the Church, to provide the Church with objective precision regarding the content of its faith, and it necessarily relies on the existence and correct exercise of the *sensus fidelium*. The latter is not just an object of attention for theologians, it constitutes a foundation and a locus for their work.[100] Theology itself, therefore, has a

---

[97] VATICAN I, *Pastor Aeternus*, ch.4 (DH 3074).

[98] See above, §40.

[99] See above, §§38, 42.

[100] Cf. ITC, *Theology Today*, §35.

two-fold relationship to the *sensus fidelium*. On the one hand, theologians depend on the *sensus fidei* because the faith that they study and articulate lives in the people of God. In this sense, theology must place itself in the school of the *sensus fidelium* so as to discover there the profound resonances of the word of God. On the other hand, theologians help the faithful to express the authentic *sensus fidelium* by reminding them of the essential lines of faith, and helping them to avoid deviations and confusion caused by the influence of imaginative elements from elsewhere. This two-fold relationship needs some clarification, as in the following sections (a) and (b).

a) Theologians depend on the sensus fidelium

82. By placing itself in the school of the *sensus fidelium*, theology steeps itself in the reality of the apostolic Tradition which underlies and overflows the strict bounds of the statements in which the teaching of the Church is formulated, because it comprises 'all that she herself is, all that she believes'.[101] In this regard, three particular considerations arise:

i) Theology should strive to detect the word which is growing like a seed in the earth of the lives of the people of God, and, having determined that a particular accent, desire or attitude does indeed come from the Spirit, and so corresponds to the *sensus fidelium*, it should integrate it into its research.

ii) By means of the *sensus fidelium*, the people of God intuitively senses what in a multitude of ideas and doctrines presented to it actually corresponds to the Gospel, and can therefore be received. Theology should apply itself carefully to investigating the various levels of reception that occur in the life of the people of God.

iii) The *sensus fidelium* both gives rise to and recognises the authenticity of the symbolic or mystical language often found in the liturgy and in popular religiosity. Aware of the manifestations of popular religiosity,[102] the theologian needs actually to participate in the life and liturgy of the local church, so as to be able to grasp in a deep way, not only with the head but also with the heart, the real context, historical and cultural, within which the Church and her members are striving to live their faith and bear witness to Christ in the world of today.

---

[101] DV 8.

[102] See below, §§107-112.

b) Theologians reflect on the sensus fidelium

83. Because the *sensus fidelium* is not simply identical to the opinion of the majority of the baptised at a given time, theology needs to provide principles and criteria for its discernment, particularly by the magisterium.[103] By critical means, theologians help to reveal and to clarify the content of the *sensus fidelium*, 'recognising and demonstrating that issues relating to the truth of faith can be complex, and that investigation of them must be precise'.[104] In this perspective, theologians should also critically examine expressions of popular piety, new currents of thought and also new movements in the Church, for the sake of fidelity to the apostolic Tradition.[105] By so doing, theologians will help the discernment of whether, in a particular case, the Church is dealing with: a deviation caused by a crisis or a misunderstanding of the faith, an opinion which has a proper place in the pluralism of the Christian community without necessarily affecting others, or something so attuned to the faith that it ought to be recognised as an inspiration or a prompting of the Spirit.

84. Theology assists the *sensus fidelium* in another way, too. It helps the faithful to know with greater clarity and precision the authentic meaning of Scripture, the true significance of conciliar definitions, the proper contents of the Tradition, and also which questions remain open – for example, because of ambiguities in current affirmations, or because of cultural factors having left their mark on what has been handed on – and in which areas a revision of previous positions is needed. The *sensus fidelium* relies on a strong and sure understanding of the faith, such as theology seeks to promote.

4. ECUMENICAL ASPECTS OF THE SENSUS FIDEI

85. The notions, *sensus fidei*, *sensus fidelium*, and *consensus fidelium*, have all been treated, or at least mentioned, in various international dialogues between the Catholic Church and other churches and ecclesial communities. Broadly speaking, there has been agreement in these dialogues that the whole body of the faithful, lay as well as ordained, bears responsibility for maintaining the Church's apostolic faith and witness, and that each of the baptised, by reason of a divine anointing (*1 Jn* 2:20, 27), has the capacity

---

[103] See below, Chapter Four.

[104] ITC, *Theology Today*, §35; cf. CDF, Instruction on the Ecclesial Vocation of the Theologian, *Donum Veritatis* (1990), nn.2-5, 6-7.

[105] Cf. *Theology Today*, §35.

to discern the truth in matters of faith. There is also general agreement that certain members of the Church exercise a special responsibility of teaching and oversight, but always in collaboration with the rest of the faithful.[106]

86. Two particular questions related to the *sensus fidelium* arise in the context of the ecumenical dialogue to which the Catholic Church is irrevocably committed:[107]

i) Should only those doctrines which gain the common consent of all Christians be regarded as expressing the *sensus fidelium* and therefore as true and binding? This proposal goes counter to the Catholic Church's faith and practice. By means of dialogue, Catholic theologians and those of other traditions seek to secure agreement on Church-dividing questions, but the Catholic participants cannot suspend their commitment to the Catholic Church's own established doctrines.

ii) Should separated Christians be understood as participating in and contributing to the *sensus fidelium* in some manner? The answer here is undoubtedly in the affirmative.[108] The Catholic Church acknowledges that 'many elements of sanctification and truth' are to be found outside her own visible bounds,[109] that 'certain features of the Christian mystery have at times been more effectively emphasised' in other communities,[110] and that ecumenical dialogue helps her to deepen and clarify her own understanding of the Gospel.

---

[106] Particularly notable in this regard are the indicated sections of the following agreed statements: Joint International Commission for Theological Dialogue between the Roman Catholic Church and the Orthodox Church, *Ecclesiological and Canonical Consequences of the Sacramental Nature of the Church: Ecclesial Communion, Conciliarity and Authority* (2007; the Ravenna Statement), n.7; Anglican-Roman Catholic International Commission, *The Gift of Authority* (1999), n.29; Evangelical-Roman Catholic Dialogue on Mission, 1977-1984, *Report*, chapter 1.3; Disciples of Christ-Roman Catholic International Commission for Dialogue, *The Church as Communion in Christ* (1992), nn.40, 45; International Commission for Dialogue between the Roman Catholic Church and the World Methodist Council, *The Word of Life* (1995), nn.56, 58.

[107] Cf. POPE JOHN PAUL II, Encyclical Letter, *Ut Unum Sint* (1995), n.3.

[108] See above, §56.

[109] Cf. LG 8.

[110] *Ut Unum Sint*, n.14; cf. nn.28, 57, where Pope John Paul refers to the 'exchange of gifts' that occurs in ecumenical dialogue. In its Letter to the Bishops of the Catholic Church on Some Aspects of the Church Understood as Communion, *Communionis Notio* (1992), the CDF similarly acknowledges that the Catholic Church is herself 'injured' by the loss of communion with the other Christian Churches and ecclesial communities (n.17).

CHAPTER FOUR

HOW TO DISCERN AUTHENTIC MANIFESTATIONS OF THE SENSUS FIDEI

87. The *sensus fidei* is essential to the life of the Church, and it is necessary now to consider how to discern and identify authentic manifestations of the *sensus fidei*. Such a discernment is particularly required in situations of tension when the authentic *sensus fidei* needs to be distinguished from expressions simply of popular opinion, particular interests or the spirit of the age. Recognising that the *sensus fidei* is an ecclesial reality in which individual believers participate, the first part of this chapter seeks to identify those characteristics which are required of the baptised if they are truly to be subjects of the *sensus fidei*, in other words, the dispositions necessary for believers to participate authentically in the *sensus fidelium*. The criteriology offered in the first part is then supplemented by consideration of the practical application of criteria with regard to the *sensus fidei* in the second part of the chapter. Part two considers three important topics: first, the close relationship between the *sensus fidei* and popular religiosity; then, the necessary distinction between the *sensus fidei* and public opinion inside or outside the Church; and, finally, the question of how to consult the faithful in matters of faith and morals.

1. DISPOSITIONS NEEDED FOR AUTHENTIC PARTICIPATION IN THE SENSUS FIDEI

88. There is not one simple disposition, but rather a set of dispositions, influenced by ecclesial, spiritual, and ethical factors. No single one can be discussed in an isolated manner; its relationship to each and all of the others has to be taken into account. Only the most important dispositions for authentic participation in the *sensus fidei* are indicated below, drawn from biblical, historical and systematic investigation, and formulated so as to be useful in practical situations of discernment.

a) Participation in the life of the Church

89. The first and most fundamental disposition is active participation in the life of the Church. Formal membership of the Church is not enough. Participation in the life of the Church means constant prayer (cf. *1 Thess* 5:17), active participation in the liturgy, especially the Eucharist, regular reception of the sacrament of reconciliation, discernment and exercise of gifts and charisms received from the Holy Spirit, and active engagement in the Church's mission and in her *diakonia*. It presumes an acceptance of the Church's teaching on matters of faith and morals, a willingness to follow the commands of God, and courage both to correct one's brothers and sisters, and also to accept correction oneself.

90. There are countless ways in which such participation may occur, but what is common in all cases is an active solidarity with the Church, coming from the heart, a feeling of fellowship with other members of the faithful and with the Church as a whole, and an instinct thereby for what the needs of and dangers to the Church are. The necessary attitude is conveyed by the expression, *sentire cum ecclesia*, to feel, sense and perceive in harmony with the Church. This is required not just of theologians, but of all the faithful; it unites all the members of the people of God as they make their pilgrim journey. It is the key to their 'walking together'.

91. The subjects of the *sensus fidei* are members of the Church who participate in the life of the Church, knowing that 'we, who are many, are one body in Christ, and individually we are members one of another' (*Rm* 12:5).

b) Listening to the word of God

92. Authentic participation in the *sensus fidei* relies necessarily on a profound and attentive listening to the word of God. Because the Bible is the original testimony of the word of God, which is handed down from generation to generation in the community of faith,[111] coherence to Scripture and Tradition is the main indicator of such listening. The *sensus fidei* is the appreciation of the faith by which the people of God 'receives not the mere word of men, but truly the word of God'.[112]

---

[111] Cf. LG 12; DV 8.
[112] LG 12, with reference to 1 Th 2:13.

93. It is not at all required that all members of the people of God should study the Bible and the witnesses of Tradition in a scientific way. Rather, what is required is an attentive and receptive listening to the Scriptures in the liturgy, and a heartfelt response, 'Thanks be to God' and 'Glory to you, Lord Jesus Christ', an eager confession of the mystery of faith, and an 'Amen' which responds to the 'Yes' God has said to his people in Jesus Christ (*2 Co* 1:20). Participation in the liturgy is the key to participation in the living Tradition of the Church, and solidarity with the poor and needy opens the heart to recognise the presence and the voice of Christ (cf. *Mt* 25:31-46).

94. The subjects of the *sensus fidei* are members of the Church who have 'received the word with joy inspired by the Holy Spirit' (*1 Th* 1:6).

c) Openness to reason

95. A fundamental disposition required for authentic participation in the *sensus fidei* is acceptance of the proper role of reason in relation to faith. Faith and reason belong together.[113] Jesus taught that God is to be loved not only 'with all your heart, and with all your soul, ... and with all your strength', but also 'with all your mind [*nous*]' (*Mk* 12:30). Because there is only one God, there is only one truth, recognised from different points of view and in different ways by faith and by reason, respectively. Faith purifies reason and widens its scope, and reason purifies faith and clarifies its coherence.[114]

96. The subjects of the *sensus fidei* are members of the Church who celebrate 'reasonable worship' and accept the proper role of reason illuminated by faith in their beliefs and practices. All the faithful are called to be 'transformed by the renewing of your minds, so that you may discern what is the will of God – what is good and acceptable and perfect' (*Rm* 12:1-2).

d) Adherence to the magisterium

97. A further disposition necessary for authentic participation in the *sensus fidei* is attentiveness to the magisterium of the Church, and a willingness

---

[113] Cf. POPE JOHN PAUL II, Encyclical Letter, *Fides et Ratio* (1998).
[114] Cf. ITC, *Theology Today*, §§63, 64, 84.

to listen to the teaching of the pastors of the Church, as an act of freedom and deeply held conviction.[115] The magisterium is rooted in the mission of Jesus, and especially in his own teaching authority (cf. *Mt* 7:29). It is intrinsically related both to Scripture and Tradition; none of these three can 'stand without the others'.[116]

98. The subjects of the *sensus fidei* are members of the Church who heed the words of Jesus to the envoys he sends: 'Whoever listens to you listens to me, and whoever rejects you rejects me, and whoever rejects me rejects the one who sent me' (*Lk* 10:16).

e) Holiness – humility, freedom and joy

99. Authentic participation in the *sensus fidei* requires holiness. Holiness is the vocation of the whole Church and of every believer.[117] To be holy fundamentally means to belong to God in Jesus Christ and in his Church, to be baptised and to live the faith in the power of the Holy Spirit. Holiness is, indeed, participation in the life of God, Father, Son and Holy Spirit, and it holds together love of God and love of neighbour, obedience to the will of God and engagement in favour of one's fellow human beings. Such a life is sustained by the Holy Spirit, who is repeatedly invoked and received by Christians (cf. *Rm* 1:7-8, 11), particularly in the liturgy.

100. In the history of the Church, the saints are the light-bearers of the *sensus fidei*. Mary, Mother of God, the All-Holy (*Panagia*), in her total acceptance of the word of God is the very model of faith and Mother of the Church.[118] Treasuring the words of Christ in her heart (*Lk* 2:51) and singing the praises of God's work of salvation (*Lk* 1:46-55), she perfectly exemplifies the delight in God's word and eagerness to proclaim the good news that the *sensus fidei* produces in the hearts of believers. In all succeeding generations, the gift of the Spirit to the Church has produced a rich harvest of holiness, and the full number of the saints is known only to God.[119] Those who are beatified and canonised stand as visible models of

---

[115] See above, §§74-80.

[116] DV 10.

[117] Cf. LG, chapter 5, on 'The universal vocation to holiness in the Church'.

[118] CCC 963.

[119] Cf. GS 11, 22.

52

Christian faith and life. For the Church, Mary and all holy persons, with their prayer and their passion, are outstanding witnesses of the *sensus fidei* in their own time and for all times, in their own place and for all places.

101. Because it fundamentally requires an *imitatio Christi* (cf. *Ph* 2:5-8), holiness essentially involves humility. Such humility is the very opposite of uncertainty or timidity; it is an act of spiritual freedom. Therefore openness (*parrhesia*) after the pattern of Christ himself (cf. *Jn* 18:20) is connected with humility and a characteristic of the *sensus fidei* as well. The first place to practice humility is within the Church itself. It is not only a virtue of lay people in relation to their pastors, but also a duty of pastors themselves in the exercise of their ministry for the Church. Jesus taught the twelve: 'Whoever wants to be first must be last of all and servant of all' (*Mk* 9:35). Humility is lived by habitually acknowledging the truth of faith, the ministry of pastors, and the needs of the faithful, especially the weakest.

102. A true indicator of holiness is 'peace and joy in the Holy Spirit' (*Rm* 14:17; cf. *1 Th* 1:6). These are gifts manifested primarily on a spiritual, not a psychological or emotional, level, namely, the peace of heart and quiet joy of the person who has found the treasure of salvation, the pearl of great price (cf. *Mt* 13:44-46). Peace and joy are, indeed, two of the most characteristic fruits of the Holy Spirit (cf. *Ga* 5:22). It is the Holy Spirit who moves the heart and turns it to God, 'opening the eyes of the mind and giving "joy and ease to everyone in assenting to the truth and believing it [*omnibus suavitatem in consentiendo et credendo veritati*]"'.[120] Joy is the opposite of the bitterness and wrath that grieve the Holy Spirit (cf. *Ep* 4:31), and is the hallmark of salvation.[121] St Peter urges Christians to rejoice in sharing Christ's sufferings, 'so that you may also be glad and shout for joy when his glory is revealed' (*1 Pt* 4:13).

103. The subjects of the *sensus fidei* are members of the Church who hear and respond to the urging of St Paul: 'make my joy complete: be of the same mind, having the same love, being in full accord and of one mind'. 'Do nothing from selfish ambition or conceit, but in humility regard others as better than yourselves' (*Ph* 2:2-3).

---

[120] DV 5 (amended translation).

[121] Cf. Pope Francis, *Evangelii Gaudium*, n.5.

f) Seeking the edification of the Church

104. An authentic manifestation of the *sensus fidei* contributes to the edification of the Church as one body, and does not foster division and particularism within her. In the first letter to the Corinthians, the very essence of participation in the life and mission of the Church is such edification (cf. *1 Co* 14). Edification means building up the Church both in the inner consciousness of its faith and in terms of new members, who want to be baptised into the faith of the Church. The Church is the house of God, a holy temple, made up of the faithful who have received the Holy Spirit (cf. *1 Co* 3:10-17). To build the Church means seeking to discover and develop one's own gifts and helping others to discover and develop their charisms, too, correcting their failures, and accepting correction oneself, in a spirit of Christian charity, working with others and praying with them, sharing their joys and sorrows (cf. *1 Co* 12:12, 26).

105. The subjects of the *sensus fidei* are members of the Church who reflect what St Paul says to the Corinthians: 'To each is given the manifestation of the Spirit for the common good' (*1 Co* 12:7).

2. APPLICATIONS

106. Discussion of dispositions appropriate to the *sensus fidei* needs to be supplemented with consideration of some important practical and pastoral questions, regarding, in particular, the relationship between the *sensus fidei* and popular religiosity; the necessary distinction between the *sensus fidei*, on the one hand, and public or majority opinion, on the other; and how to consult the faithful in matters of faith and morals. These points will now be considered in turn.

a) The sensus fidei and popular religiosity

107. There is a 'religiosity' that is natural for human beings; religious questions naturally arise in every human life, prompting a vast diversity of religious beliefs and popular practices, and the phenomenon of popular religiosity has been the object of much attention and study in recent times.[122]

---

[122] Cf. Congregation for Divine Worship and the Discipline of the Sacraments (CDWDS), *Directory on Popular Piety and the Liturgy: Principles and Guidelines* (2001), n.10: '"Popular religiosity" refers to a universal experience: there is always a religious dimension in the hearts of people, nations, and their collective expressions. All peoples tend to give expression to their totalising view of the transcendent, their concept of nature, society, and history through cultic means. Such characteristic syntheses are of major spiritual and human importance.'

108. 'Popular religiosity' also has a more specific usage, namely in reference to the great variety of manifestations of Christian belief found among the people of God in the Church, or, rather, to refer to 'the Catholic wisdom of the people' that finds expression in such a multitude of ways. That wisdom 'creatively combines the divine and the human, Christ and Mary, spirit and body, communion and institution, person and community, faith and homeland, intelligence and emotion', and is also for the people 'a principle of discernment and an evangelical instinct through which they spontaneously sense when the Gospel is served in the Church and when it is emptied of its content and stifled by other interests'.[123] As such a wisdom, principle and instinct, popular religiosity is clearly very closely related to the *sensus fidei*, and needs to be considered carefully within the framework of the present study.

109. The words of Jesus, 'I thank you, Father, Lord of heaven and earth, because you have hidden these things from the wise and the intelligent and have revealed them to infants' (*Mt* 11:25; *Lk* 10:21), are highly relevant in this context. They indicate the wisdom and insight into the things of God that is given to those of humble faith. Vast multitudes of humble Christian believers (and indeed of people beyond the visible bounds of the Church) have privileged access, at least potentially, to the deep truths of God. Popular religiosity arises in particular from the knowledge of God vouchsafed to such people. It is 'the manifestation of a theological life nourished by the working of the Holy Spirit who has been poured into our hearts (cf. *Rm* 5:5)'.[124]

110. Both as a principle or instinct and as a rich abundance of Christian practice, especially in the form of cultic activities, e.g. devotions, pilgrimages and processions, popular religiosity springs from and makes manifest the *sensus fidei*, and is to be respected and fostered. It needs to be recognised that popular piety, in particular, is 'the first and most fundamental form of faith's "inculturation"'.[125] Such piety is 'an ecclesial

---

[123] CELAM, Third General Conference (Puebla, 1979), Final Document, n.448, as quoted in CCC 1676.

[124] Pope Francis, *Evangelii Gaudium*, n.125.

[125] Joseph Ratzinger, *Commento teologico*, in Congregation for the Doctrine of the Faith, *Il messaggio di Fatima* (Libreria Editrice Vaticana, Città del Vaticano, 2000), p.35; as quoted in CDWDS, *Directory*, n.91.

reality prompted and guided by the Holy Spirit',[126] by whom the people of God are indeed anointed as a 'holy priesthood'. It is natural for the priesthood of the people to find expression in a multitude of ways.

111. The priestly activity of the people rightly has its high point in the liturgy, and care must be taken to ensure that popular devotions 'accord with the sacred liturgy'.[127] More generally, as Pope Paul VI taught, since it is in danger of being penetrated 'by many distortions of religion and even superstitions', popular religiosity needs to be evangelised.[128] However, when carefully tended in this way, and 'well oriented', it is, he said, 'rich in values'. 'It manifests a thirst for God which only the simple and poor can know. It makes people capable of generosity and sacrifice even to the point of heroism, when it is a question of manifesting belief. It involves an acute awareness of profound attributes of God: fatherhood, providence, living and constant presence. It engenders interior attitudes rarely observed to the same degree elsewhere: patience, the sense of the Cross in daily life, detachment, openness to others, devotion.... When it is well oriented, this popular religiosity can be more and more for multitudes of our people a true encounter with God in Jesus Christ.'[129] In admiring the elderly woman's statement,[130] Pope Francis was echoing the esteem expressed here by Pope Paul. Once again, well oriented popular religiosity, both in its insight into the deep mysteries of the Gospel and in its courageous witness of faith, can be seen as a manifestation and expression of the *sensus fidei*.

---

[126] CDWDS, *Directory*, n.50.

[127] SC 13.

[128] POPE PAUL VI, Apostolic Exhortation, *Evangelii Nuntiandi* (1975), n.48. Congar referred to 'engouements douteux et dévotions aberrantes', and cautioned: 'On se gardera de trop attribuer au *sensus fidelium*: non seulement au regard des prérogatives de la hiérarchie ..., mais en soi' (*Jalons pour une théologie du laïcat*, p.399; ET, *Lay People in the Church*, p.288).

[129] POPE PAUL VI, Apostolic Exhortation, *Evangelii Nuntiandi* (1975), n.48. In his discourse at the opening of CELAM's fourth general conference (Santo Domingo, 12 October 1992), Pope John Paul said that, with its 'essentially catholic roots', popular religiosity in Latin America was 'an antidote against the sects and a guarantee of fidelity to the message of salvation' (n.12). With reference to the Final Document of the Third General Conference of CELAM, Pope Francis states that, when the Christian faith is truly inculturated, 'popular piety' is an important part of the process by which 'a people continuously evangelises itself' (*Evangelii Gaudium*, n.122).

[130] See above, §2.

112. It may be said that popular religiosity is 'well oriented' when it is truly 'ecclesial'. Pope Paul indicated in the same text certain criteria for ecclesiality. Being ecclesial means being nourished by the Word of God, not being politicised or trapped by ideologies, remaining strongly in communion with both the local church and the universal Church, with the Church's pastors and with the magisterium, and being fervently missionary.[131] These criteria indicate conditions required for the authenticity both of popular religiosity and of the *sensus fidei* that underlies it. In their authentic form, as the final criterion indicates, both are great resources for the Church's mission. Pope Francis highlights the 'missionary power' of popular piety, and in what can be seen as a reference to the *sensus fidei*, states that 'underlying popular piety' there is likewise 'an active evangelising power which we must not underestimate: to do so would be to fail to recognise the work of the Holy Spirit'.[132]

b) The sensus fidei and public opinion

113. One of the most delicate topics is the relationship between the *sensus fidei* and public or majority opinion both inside and outside the Church. Public opinion is a sociological concept, which applies first of all to political societies. The emergence of public opinion is linked to the birth and development of the political model of representative democracy. In so far as political power gains its legitimacy from the people, the latter must make known their thoughts, and political power must take account of them in the exercise of government. Public opinion is therefore essential to the healthy functioning of democratic life, and it is important that it be enlightened and informed in a competent and honest manner. That is the role of the mass media, which thus contribute greatly to the common good of society, as long as they do not seek to manipulate opinion in favour of particular interests.

114. The Church appreciates the high human and moral values espoused by democracy, but she herself is not structured according to the principles of a secular political society. The Church, the mystery of the communion of humanity with God, receives her constitution from Christ. It is from him

---

[131] Cf. POPE PAUL VI, *Evangelii Nuntiandi*, n.58; with reference to the need to ensure that *communautés de base* were truly ecclesial.

[132] POPE FRANCIS, *Evangelii Gaudium*, n.126.

that she receives her internal structure and her principles of government. Public opinion cannot, therefore, play in the Church the determinative role that it legitimately plays in the political societies that rely on the principle of popular sovereignty, though it does have a proper role in the Church, as we shall seek to clarify below.

115. The mass media comment frequently on religious affairs. Public interest in matters of faith is a good sign, and the freedom of the press is a basic human right. The Catholic Church is not afraid of discussion or controversy regarding her teaching. On the contrary, she welcomes debate as a manifestation of religious freedom. Everyone is free either to criticise or to support her. Indeed, she recognises that fair and constructive critique can help her to see problems more clearly and to find better solutions. She herself, in turn, is free to criticise unfair attacks, and needs access to the media in order to defend the faith if necessary. She values invitations from independent media to contribute to public debates. She does not want a monopoly of information, but appreciates the plurality and interchange of opinions. She also, however, knows the importance of informing society about the true meaning and content both of her faith and of her moral teaching.

116. The voices of lay people are heard much more frequently now in the Church, sometimes with conservative and sometimes with progressive positions, but generally participating constructively in the life and the mission of the Church. The huge development of society by education has had considerable impact on relations within the Church. The Church herself is engaged worldwide in educational programmes aimed at giving people their own voice and their own rights. It is therefore a good sign if many people today are interested in the teaching, the liturgy and the service of the Church. Many members of the Church want to exercise their own competence, and to participate in their own proper way in the life of the Church. They organise themselves within parishes and in various groups and movements to build up the Church and to influence society at large, and they seek contact via social media with other believers and with people of good will.

117. The new networks of communication both inside and outside the Church call for new forms of attention and critique, and the renewal of skills of discernment. There are influences from special interest groups which are not compatible, or not fully so, with the Catholic faith; there are

convictions which are only applicable to a certain place or time; and there are pressures to lessen the role of faith in public debate or to accommodate traditional Christian doctrine to modern concerns and opinions.

118. It is clear that there can be no simple identification between the *sensus fidei* and public or majority opinion. These are by no means the same thing.

i) First of all, the *sensus fidei* is obviously related to faith, and faith is a gift not necessarily possessed by all people, so the *sensus fidei* can certainly not be likened to public opinion in society at large. Then also, while Christian faith is, of course, the primary factor uniting members of the Church, many different influences combine to shape the views of Christians living in the modern world. As the above discussion of dispositions implicitly shows, the *sensus fidei* cannot simply be identified, therefore, with public or majority opinion in the Church, either. Faith, not opinion, is the necessary focus of attention. Opinion is often just an expression, frequently changeable and transient, of the mood or desires of a certain group or culture, whereas faith is the echo of the one Gospel which is valid for all places and times.

ii) In the history of the people of God, it has often been not the majority but rather a minority which has truly lived and witnessed to the faith. The Old Testament knew the 'holy remnant' of believers, sometimes very few in number, over against the kings and priests and most of the Israelites. Christianity itself started as a small minority, blamed and persecuted by public authorities. In the history of the Church, evangelical movements such as the Franciscans and Dominicans, or later the Jesuits, started as small groups treated with suspicion by various bishops and theologians. In many countries today, Christians are under strong pressure from other religions or secular ideologies to neglect the truth of faith and weaken the boundaries of ecclesial community. It is therefore particularly important to discern and listen to the voices of the 'little ones who believe' (*Mk* 9:42).

119. It is undoubtedly necessary to distinguish between the *sensus fidei* and public or majority opinion, hence the need to identify dispositions necessary for participation in the *sensus fidei*, such as those elaborated above. Nevertheless, it is the whole people of God which, in its inner unity, confesses and lives the true faith. The magisterium and theology

must work constantly to renew the presentation of the faith in different
situations, confronting if necessary dominant notions of Christian truth
with the actual truth of the Gospel, but it must be recalled that the
experience of the Church shows that sometimes the truth of the faith has
been conserved not by the efforts of theologians or the teaching of the
majority of bishops but in the hearts of believers.

c) Ways of consulting the faithful

120. There is a genuine equality of dignity among all the faithful, because
through their baptism they are all reborn in Christ. 'Because of this
equality they all contribute, each according to his or her own condition
and office, to the building up of the Body of Christ.'[133] Therefore, all the
faithful 'have the right, indeed at times the duty, in keeping with their
knowledge, competence and position, to manifest to the sacred Pastors
their views on matters which concern the good of the Church'. 'They
have the right to make their views known to others of Christ's faithful,
but in doing so they must always respect the integrity of faith and morals,
show due reference to the Pastors and take into account both the common
good and the dignity of individuals.'[134] Accordingly, the faithful, and
specifically the lay people, should be treated by the Church's pastors with
respect and consideration, and consulted in an appropriate way for the
good of the Church.

121. The word 'consult' includes the idea of seeking a judgement or advice
as well as inquiring into a matter of fact. On the one hand, in matters of
governance and pastoral issues, the pastors of the Church can and should
consult the faithful in certain cases in the sense of asking for their advice
or their judgement. On the other hand, when the magisterium is defining
a doctrine, it is appropriate to consult the faithful in the sense of inquiring
into a matter of fact, 'because the body of the faithful is one of the
witnesses to the fact of the tradition of revealed doctrine, and because their
consensus through Christendom is the voice of the Infallible Church'.[135]

---

[133] Code of Canon Law, can.208.

[134] Code of Canon Law, can.212, §3.

[135] NEWMAN, *On Consulting the Faithful*, p.63; for the double meaning of the word 'consult',
see pp.54-55.

122. The practice of consulting the faithful is not new in the life of the Church. In the medieval Church a principle of Roman law was used: *Quod omnes tangit, ab omnibus tractari et approbari debet* (what affects everyone, should be discussed and approved by all). In the three domains of the life of the Church (faith, sacraments, governance), 'tradition combined a hierarchical structure with a concrete regime of association and agreement', and this was considered to be an 'apostolic practice' or an 'apostolic tradition'.[136]

123. Problems arise when the majority of the faithful remain indifferent to doctrinal or moral decisions taken by the magisterium or when they positively reject them. This lack of reception may indicate a weakness or a lack of faith on the part of the people of God, caused by an insufficiently critical embrace of contemporary culture. But in some cases it may indicate that certain decisions have been taken by those in authority without due consideration of the experience and the *sensus fidei* of the faithful, or without sufficient consultation of the faithful by the magisterium.[137]

124. It is only natural that there should be a constant communication and regular dialogue on practical issues and matters of faith and morals between members of the Church. Public opinion is an important form of that communication in the Church. 'Since the Church is a living body, she needs public opinion in order to sustain a giving and taking between her members. Without this, she cannot advance in thought and action.'[138] This endorsement of a public exchange of thought and opinions in the Church was given soon after Vatican II, precisely on the basis of the council's teaching on the *sensus fidei* and on Christian love, and the faithful were strongly encouraged to take an active part in that public exchange. 'Catholics should be fully aware of the real freedom to speak their minds which stems from a "feeling for the faith" [i.e. the *sensus fidei*] and from love. It stems from that feeling for the faith which is aroused and

---

[136] Y. CONGAR, 'Quod omnes tangit, ab omnibus tractari et approbari debet', in *Revue historique de droit français et étranger* 36 (1958), pp.210-259, esp. pp.224-228.

[137] See above, §§78-80.

[138] Pastoral Instruction on the Means of Social Communication written by Order of the Second Vatican Council, *'Communio et Progressio'* (1971), n.115, which also cites Pope Pius XII: 'Something would be lacking in [the Church's] life if she had no public opinion. Both pastors of souls and lay people would be to blame for this' (Allocution, 17 February 1950, AAS XVIII[1950], p.256).

nourished by the spirit of truth in order that, under the guidance of the teaching Church which they accept with reverence, the People of God may cling unswervingly to the faith given to the early Church, with true judgement penetrate its meaning more deeply, and apply it more fully in their lives [*Lumen Gentium*, 12]. This freedom also stems from love. For it is with love that ... the People of God are raised to an intimate sharing in the freedom of Christ Himself, who cleansed us from our sins, in order that we might be able freely to make judgements in accordance with the will of God. Those who exercise authority in the Church will take care to ensure that there is responsible exchange of freely held and expressed opinion among the People of God. More than this, they will set up norms and conditions for this to take place.'[139]

125. Such public exchange of opinion is a prime means by which, in a normal way, the *sensus fidelium* can be gauged. Since the Second Vatican Council, however, various institutional instruments by which the faithful may more formally be heard and consulted have been established, such as particular councils, to which priests and others of Christ's faithful may be invited,[140] diocesan synods, to which the diocesan bishop may also invite lay people as members,[141] the pastoral council of each diocese, which is 'composed of members of Christ's faithful who are in full communion with the Catholic Church: clerics, members of institutes of consecrated life, and especially lay people',[142] and pastoral councils in parishes, in which 'Christ's faithful, together with those who by virtue of their office are engaged in pastoral care in the parish, give their help in fostering pastoral action'.[143]

126. Structures of consultation such as those mentioned above can be greatly beneficial to the Church, but only if pastors and lay people are mutually respectful of one another's charisms and if they carefully and continually listen to one another's experiences and concerns. Humble listening at all levels and proper consultation of those concerned are integral aspects of a living and lively Church.

---

[139] '*Communio et Progressio*', n.116.

[140] Cf. *Code of Canon Law*, can.443, §4.

[141] Cf. *Code of Canon Law*, can.463, §2.

[142] *Code of Canon Law*, can.512, §1.

[143] *Code of Canon Law*, can.536, §1.

CONCLUSION

127. Vatican II was a new Pentecost,[144] equipping the Church for the new evangelisation that popes since the council have called for. The council gave a renewed emphasis to the traditional idea that all of the baptised have a *sensus fidei*, and the *sensus fidei* constitutes a most important resource for the new evangelisation.[145] By means of the *sensus fidei*, the faithful are able not only to recognise what is in accordance with the Gospel and to reject what is contrary to it, but also to sense what Pope Francis has called 'new ways for the journey' in faith of the whole pilgrim people. One of the reasons why bishops and priests need to be close to their people on the journey and to walk with them is precisely so as to recognise 'new ways' as they are sensed by the people.[146] The discernment of such new ways, opened up and illumined by the Holy Spirit, will be vital for the new evangelisation.

128. The *sensus fidei* is closely related to the *'infallibilitas in credendo'* that the Church as a whole has as a believing 'subject' making its pilgrim way in history.[147] Sustained by the Holy Spirit, it enables the witness that the Church gives and the discernment that the members of the Church must constantly make, both as individuals and as a community, of how best to live and act and speak in fidelity to the Lord. It is the instinct by which each and all 'think with the Church',[148] sharing one faith and one purpose. It is what unites pastors and people, and makes dialogue between them, based on their respective gifts and callings, both essential and fruitful for the Church.

---

[144] This was a phrase repeatedly used by Pope John XXIII when he expressed his hopes and prayers for the coming council; see, e.g., Apostolic Constitution, *Humanae Salutis* (1961), n.23.

[145] Cf. above, §§2, 45, 65, 70, 112.

[146] Cf. POPE FRANCIS, Address to clergy, persons in consecrated life and members of pastoral councils, San Rufino, Assisi, 4 October 2013. The pope added that diocesan synods, particular celebrations of 'walking together' as disciples of the Lord, need to take account of 'what the Holy Spirit is saying to the laity, to the people of God, [and] to all'.

[147] Interview with Pope Francis by Fr Antonio Spadaro, 21 September 2013; cf. POPE FRANCIS, *Evangelii Gaudium*, n.119.

[148] Interview with Pope Francis by Fr Antonio Spadaro; cf. above, §90.